D1575747

Value Analysis for Better Management

Value Analysis
for Better Management

Warren J. Ridge

American Management Association, Inc.

Standard book number: 8144-5193-4

Library of Congress catalog card number: 75-96142

First printing

To my wife, Joan, and my daughter, Diane.
Their understanding, assistance, and sense of humor
made this production almost enjoyable.

Acknowledgments

D<small>URING</small> the four years spent in developing these concepts into a practical and usable form, I was fortunate indeed to have had some of the best assistance available. Everett A. Lindem, an outstanding value engineering educator, spent many hours with me in designing the workshop seminar. Our subsequent success with the seminar gave evidence of Everett's expertise. Edward D. Heller, one of the nation's foremost authorities on value engineering, constantly prodded me to continue when it would have been so easy to quit. His contribution to this discipline was substantial, and his belief in the concepts removed many of my roadblocks. George J. Bartolomei was my frequent adviser. George, the most creative individual I've met and a nationally acknowledged value engineering expert, contributed much to sharpening the original ideas. John P. Fowler, a noted authority on municipal operations and other forms of institutional organizations, helped expand the parameters of application beyond those originally established. Nate L. Dickinson had the managerial foresight to recognize the value of these precepts, and his innovative application of the techniques will, I am sure, provide the basis for additional chapters in future revisions. To these individuals I am deeply indebted.

W<small>ARREN</small> J. R<small>IDGE</small>

Introduction

Many managers eagerly seek the talisman that, with little effort, will provide a panacea for all management ills. Unfortunately, this book will not conclude their search. Neither does it contain effortless solutions. It does describe a unique integration of techniques that constitutes an effective process for optimizing the value of organization and paperwork. It is an extremely flexible procedure that can be applied at all levels of management. It can be used by the first-line supervisor to increase the efficiency of his group, and it can be used by the company president as a basis for major reorganization.

The techniques were designed specifically to combat the much-publicized growth of paperwork. But, since paperwork is usually the product of an organization, the scope had to be expanded to accommodate a functional evaluation of that slippery concept—organization. These two areas, paperwork and organization, contribute significantly to the total cost of business and deserve considerable attention in the quest for profit improvement.

In addition to the direct, measurable advantages of this discipline, there are several corollary benefits. Its use promotes realistic program planning at the levels of application; establishes work standards in the indirect areas; provides effective training features; and, most important, tends to increase employee morale and interdepartmental co-operation.

This book is directed to all echelons of management—to the generalist as well as the specialist. It is not the magic potion that will per se attain the ultimate in cost reduction. It requires hard work and an investment, but the potential rewards far exceed those of any other management device.

Contents

Exhibits

Value Analysis for Better Management

I

The Paperwork Menace

In 1908, President Theodore Roosevelt tried to combat the paperwork menace by issuing Executive Order No. 937, which created the Interdepartmental Statistical Committee. The purpose of this committee was to suggest ways to eliminate unnecessary duplication of work and conflicting results. But even a big stick was no match for such a powerful adversary. The attempt failed. Some 60 years later the menace not only exists but has grown during this period to gargantuan proportions. Many other investigations and assaults were relatively ineffective and resulted merely in reidentifying the menace and portending disaster. It appeared that neither government nor industry had the capability to curb the paperwork inundation.

Recently, a 70-page report was published by the House Post Office and Civil Service Subcommittee that highlighted the magnitude of government paperwork. The report stated that federal agencies require 15 billion copies of 360,000 forms to conduct their business for one year, and somewhere there are 225,000 people tucking these documents into 25 million cubic feet of files. The Executive offices alone have two million file cabinets. Also, the government spends $1.5 billion each year producing a billion letters. Indeed, if one government record were burned each second, it would take more than 2,000 years to destroy them all.

Few industrial managers are likely to be shocked by these statistics because bureaucracy has always carried the stigma of inefficiency. The manager many times has complained that the federal paperwork jungle is too costly and too large. "Why don't they operate their business as I do mine, especially since I'm paying for this waste out of my pocket? Why can't they be a little more frugal with my money?"

But is the paperwork deluge a problem only for Uncle Sam or might the average stockholder have reason to voice the same complaints? In January 1968 the New York Stock Exchange began to sag under the pressure of paperwork. The board of governors suspended all trading on Wednesdays to "catch up on stockpiled paperwork." When this failed to reduce the pressure, the board took a new tack; it ordered resumption of the five-day trading week but shortened the trading day. Still the problems were not resolved and the paperwork menace continued. Not since the crash of 1929 had the market been compelled to curtail operations so significantly. Paperwork accomplished what international gold manipulations could not do, what the impact of global wars failed to do, and what natural disasters never have been able to do.

Stock exchanges and brokerage houses throughout the country can attest to the tremendous losses caused by paperwork, and this can be logically applied to industry in general. It is estimated that the annual paperwork cost to industry approaches $120 billion, or about one-seventh of the total national production of goods and services.

The documents that are being typed, mailed, and filed daily are of course created by people, and these people usually belong to something called an organization. So it may be said that the organization is the efficient cause of paperwork cost. But regardless of the cause, it is impractical to evaluate economy in this area without examining paperwork's interdependence with the organization.

In order to evaluate the worth of the expensive mass of paperwork in industry and government and, hopefully, to reduce its present impact on the cost of operations, a new management discipline is needed. Previous efforts have failed to provide a meaningful method of paperwork and organization evaluation. The principles and techniques described in this book were developed to fulfill this need. Although leaning heavily on value engineering, this new discipline is not pure value engineering. Although borrowing some techniques of work simplification, it cannot be classed as work simplification. It is a hybrid that is far more effective than the techniques from which it is derived.

Before exploring the realm of value analysis of management practices (VAMP), let us examine the significant causes of paperwork generation and other factors contributing to paperwork growth. This cursory examination, coupled with a brief description of past and present attempts to reduce paperwork, will afford a better understanding of the expanse of paperwork costs and the requirement for a new approach.

CAUSES OF PAPERWORK EXPANSION

An important factor in producing this mountain of paperwork is the computer, and it can rightfully claim the place of honor as one of the most effective tools in the generation of paper. It has been termed the most important technological advance of the twentieth century and probably any previous century. It can guide a space vehicle to a particular crater on the moon, it can run an entire oil refinery, and it can regulate the positioning of microelements for brain surgery, as well as control prosthetic devices. In addition to its many beneficial uses, it can and does produce paper. In 1968 there were approximately 35,000 computers in this country, each capable of spewing out a stack of records 20 feet high each day. And consider the conditions if the following projections approach reality:

- Information per se will be inexpensive and readily available.
- Large and varied data banks will exist and be accessible to the public.
- Computers will be used extensively in management science and decision making.
- Computers will be economically feasible for firms and activities of all sizes.
- Computers will process language inputs and recognize voices.
- Computers will be used extensively at all levels of government.

- Computers will increase the pace of technological development.

Each one of these expectations has an appreciable impact on paperwork and organization growth.

A conservative estimate of computer growth in this country indicates that by 1975 the number of computers will have increased by at
least a factor of 20. At that point we will have expanded our paper-
generating ability by the computer alone to such an extent that we
will be able to produce 23 stacks of records per minute, each equal in
height to the Empire State building. At this rate, one year's production of paper will be enough to construct six pillars to the moon.
Perhaps the sociologists concerned with the population explosion
should redirect their efforts. At the present rate it would appear that
the quantities of paper will displace people long before the food
supply diminishes to the critical point.

Help Through Education

Paperwork is not created by the illiterate. It begins innocently in
the fourth or fifth grade with the instruction to express one's
thoughts in writing. At first it is the 100-word theme, with emphasis
on the quantity of words rather than on their arrangement to convey
ideas. This may be necessary to force the beginner to become accus-
tomed to using words, but it continues as the student advances. Soon
100 words become 500, then 1,000; in high school, 3,000-word
themes are not uncommon. During this entire period, the important
thing is to fill the page with words.

When the student enters college, he is no longer required to count
the number of words in his term paper. All he has to do now is to
count the number of pages—a tremendous saving. Unfortunately, this
practice endures in some graduate schools, where 25 pages per credit
is considered the norm in term papers.

Even the doctoral dissertations are creating havoc for the candidate. Where a decade ago he could write on the history of California,
he now has to be content with the history of one small arroyo because
everything else has already been the topic of previous dissertations.

After the college student has mastered the art of word production, he is presented with a piece of paper which attests that he is now capable of contributing to the national stockpile of paper. The management neophyte is now exposed to industrial training programs in effective writing, technical writing, communication, and, of course, the principles of management. He is constantly admonished in these classes to write to express, not to impress. It certainly makes sense to him, so he tries. However, his first attempt may well be returned with the comment that it lacks professionalism and should be dressed up a bit.

The junior executive immediately understands the rules of this game and expertly whips up 12 pages high in fog content. His superior commends him, signs his name to the manuscript, and has 50 copies reproduced and distributed. After several attempts to understand the data, the recipient of the report eventually telephones the author for a three-minute interpretation.

The training courses offered are primarily directed at the wrong level of management. Dr. James Hayes, dean of the Duquesne University Graduate School of Business Administration, very aptly described this condition as a smorgasbord approach to industrial training. The courses are offered through the generosity of the company. Those who really don't require the training attend; those who do, bowl. In identifying the causes of the paperwork menace, managers in industry cannot be completely exonerated.

Expert's Advice

Recently, the attention given to paperwork and organization reached a new level of intensity in both foreign and domestic industry. New programs were established to combat this ogre and new surveys were undertaken to assess the current and potential damage. Work simplification and management science became the bywords. Systems that had worked well in the thirties, such as forms design, flow process charts, and report and record management guides, were reactivated.

In the wake of such popularity, new books were published, consulting firms were established, and work simplification seminars were developed to assist in highlighting the massive paperwork problem. Hardly a business periodical is published without warnings that utter chaos will ensue unless definite steps are taken to curtail the flow of paperwork. The prognostications are believable and the data are there, all pointing to certain doom.

With such well-publicized problems, the emergence of experts is axiomatic. History professor C. Northcote Parkinson formulated his laws which describe the conditions under which organization and paperwork flourish, and these laws have been widely published and widely quoted. The business manager *knows* that the cost of paperwork is excessive and all organizations are overstaffed—all, that is, except his own. He has read Parkinson and has chuckled over Parkinson's apparent clairvoyance in pointing out the excess in *other* areas. He has read other alleged experts, be they English professors, professional writers, or scientists, and he has marveled at their grasp of the situation. They all confirm that his business colleagues are, indeed, in dire need of assistance in these areas. For each article he reads that suggests ways of reducing paperwork costs, he immediately obtains a Xerox copy and dispatches it to his fellow managers.

The do-it-yourself fad has also arrived in the form of managers' self-appraisals. These questionnaires usually appear in business periodicals and are titled, for example, "Rate Yourself as a Cost-Conscious Manager." The questions are listed vertically, and to the right of each question are self-rating factors: "unsatisfactory," "satisfactory," or "excellent." Each question is worded to elicit one of the three ratings. The manager reads Question 1, "Do you utilize equipment effectively?" and circles the rating factor that describes his effectiveness in this area. He then goes on to the next question—which is as abstract as the first—rates himself, and continues.

If that were all there was to it, the questionnaire would be of value. It would at least compel the manager to be aware of equipment utilization as a cost factor along with the subjects of the other questions. But all too often these questionnaires contain a numerical measurement system that is intended to indicate whether the manager should consider himself satisfactory or otherwise in controlling costs. If his score puts him in the excellent category (and most will), he can logically deduce that his excellence obviates the need for any future attention to these cost areas.

The experts do assist by highlighting the growth of the paperwork menace, but their advice and efforts frequently fall far short of developing effective restraints.

Socioeconomic Contributions

Another factor contributing to increased paperwork is the dynamic nature of business and society, including the growth of the computer. Automation has often been accused of being the primary cause of higher unemployment rates. Yet several analyses of these causes have revealed that the computer was only one of the significant contributors. Studies of employment statistics over the past 10 to 15 years have shown that agricultural employment declined substantially during the periods covered by the studies. But during the same periods the number of people employed in service industries expanded by approximately the same percentage as agricultural employment declined.

The causes of such adjustments are ascribed to a number of agents all working together, but the identification of these agents and the assignment of responsibility is of little importance here compared to their effect on paperwork and organization. The change from agriculture to the service industries involved in this paperwork pastime individuals who never before had participated in the making of a procedure. The farm boy who never needed a requisition to back the tractor out of the barn each morning is now preparing five-part tool requests, detailed time cards, and other assorted bits of paper.

The socioeconomic change in the nature of business is of particular importance to the educator and the manager. The educator will have to provide frequent retraining and re-education for the individual to cope with economic and sociological change, and the manager will be faced with the product. In the past, the manager could refer to articles or manuals on the proper span of control which would outline, within certain tolerances, the proper ratio of workers and supervisors. He could compare his indirect-to-direct ratio with others in the same type of business, as well as follow a typical organization plan for a typical task. These data were based on history. But the very character of business is changing in unprecedented ways, so these comparisons are becoming less and less useful to the manager and the new variables that are being introduced would foil the best mathematical model maker.

The shift of workers is from unskilled, non-paper-producing employment areas to the semiskilled and skilled areas noted for paper-work addiction. The annual cost of paperwork may well increase far beyond the $120 billion estimate to a point where it equals the production of all hardware used in creating the flood. The complexity of organization caused by these changes may in the future be magni-fied several times, and our current evaluation and control methods will be too outdated to respond. Something new, something capable of facing these odds, seems to be the only answer.

HOW MUCH IS ENOUGH?

With all the studies and all the expert advice on paperwork and organization, it is generally accepted that there is too much of both. If those who decry present or future conditions in these areas have empirical knowledge of this excess, it can be concluded that they can identify the point at which one passes from sufficient to excess. Conversely, if parameters have not been established and exist in the abstract only, perhaps the historians, English professors, and profes-sional authors have not fully appraised the industrial and governmen-tal problem of paperwork and organization. In fact, there may not be a problem at all. If a problem is described as an *unwanted* effect, then by the law of implication there must be a *wanted* effect. This wanted effect can be termed the standard, norm, objective, or goal, and the degree of deviation of the actual from the standard becomes the problem. In this context, the magnitude of the paperwork problem cannot be validly assessed until the desired effects have been estab-lished and identified. There is no doubt a large quantity of paperwork —but is it excessive?

Using this definition of a problem, it would be logical to conclude that the absence of standards of performance in measuring the suffi-ciency of paperwork and organization would preclude the identifica-tion of a problem in this area and that the problem should be elevated to a higher level of abstraction. The problem would then become the absence of standards per se.

How does the manager know, when he is staffing a new element of organization, that the level he proposes has a positive correlation to the basic function of that element? He can compare it to similar organizations; he can reflect on his own experience; he can use intui-tive thinking; and, if all else fails, he can resort to the many master's theses on organization analysis in the nearby campus library. Probably in all these cases the manager will construct an organization that works and does result in a return on investment. If the return falls within the narrow range established by industrial averages, he is considered a successful manager. This is usually true even though the average may be 50 percent of maximum. It's a go, no-go type of evaluation, the pragmatic approach that anything that works is good. To the marginal manager, this condition represents a haven. But for the professional manager an appraisal system that allows him to determine the optimum staffing and also represents the maximum return on investments is invaluable.

The same analysis is applicable to procedures whether they are written or oral, prescribed or conventional. Some managers contend that the elimination of written procedures in toto would not only result in tremendous cost savings but would also increase employee efficiency and improve morale. In some instances they may be correct, but how do they know? If cost reduction per se is an end objective, then the manager who ceases business activity entirely and closes his plant wins the game. He has truly avoided all future costs and has eliminated all current costs, thereby attaining the maximum in cost reduction. This is obviously facetious, but it highlights a very important concept: The objective of cost reduction is to decrease current cost and avoid potential increases in future costs *without* a commensurate reduction in the value of the products or services the expenditures represent.

Procedures have their place. Consider the pandemonium that would exist if the Internal Revenue Service directed each citizen to submit an income tax return on April 15 of each year yet provided no guidelines, procedures, or forms for their submission. Similarly, would the manager who advocates elimination of procedures want the pilot of a commercial airliner to scrap his checklist, if the manager were tightly strapped into a seat on that particular airliner?

Procedures provide a guide for handling recurrent tasks in an efficient manner and result in the reduction of costly operational and administrative errors. The management function of planning is in itself a procedure to attempt to make things happen which, if left to chance, might not occur. Since the plan has to be controlled, procedures are necessary to insure that events conform to plans. Detractors argue that procedures inhibit creativity, restrict technical and cultural advances, and foster organizational robots. To a degree this may be true, but the value of *some* organizational conformance and *some* creative inhibition may be far greater to the businessman than its absence is to the artist, psychologist, and sociologist.

Until the abstract notions of excessiveness and sufficiency in both paperwork and organization can be assigned specific parameters, the cynic's claims involving these concepts can, at best, be considered pure conjecture.

PAST AND PRESENT ATTEMPTS

Man's earliest attempts at writing were restricted to making impressions in sand, mud, and stone, but these methods lacked permanence. However, as time passed and man constantly strove to develop ways to transfer his ideas to others, he progressed from writing on clay tablets to writing on papyrus and finally to writing on paper. Little thought was given to paper expansion or control in those days, for the efforts required to prepare manuscripts were so time consuming as to be self-restricting. With the invention of the printing press, an explosion of knowledge occurred. At last, thoughts could be recorded easily and could be disseminated widely. The invention of the typewriter abetted the growth of paperwork, but the quantities of paper produced in those eras gave no indication of the impending avalanche. Yet these two inventions, the printing press and the typewriter, are a classic example of synergy.

When the existence of the paper cannibal became evident to the farsighted in the early 1900's, techniques were developed to ward off the paper inundation. Later these techniques were embodied in the discipline of work simplification. Its emergence heralded a new dimension in industrial control and economy. The introduction of the flow process chart allowed the actions of a person or a piece of paper in the performance of a specific task to be visualized in detail, sufficient to dissect the overall task analytically. The procedure flow chart, usually less detailed than the flow process chart, was designed to describe symbolically an entire procedure and show the interrelationships of paper and people. The data are then subjected to tests that Kipling characterized as six honest serving men: what, why, where, when, how, and who. Each discrete step is examined and attempts are made to eliminate it, combine it with another step, or resequence it so that it will improve the efficiency of the procedure and reduce operating costs.

Another important work simplification technique, introduced by the Bureau of the Budget in the 1940's, is the work distribution study. Often called a department inventory study, its purpose is to indicate clearly how much and what types of work are being done and by whom. The objective of the work distribution study is work improvement through increased use of available skills, modified workload balance, proper allocation of responsibility, job enlargement, and elimination of waste. These data are collected by the individuals performing the tasks and integrated on a chart which provides an overview of the total organization's output and objectives. The most important aspect of these three instruments is the overall visualization they provide. Display of these data on wall charts normally results in increased attention by management and, on occasion, in disbelief.

Reports and records management received considerable emphasis in the early 1950's as an effective way to reduce the cost of forms and records. Another technique of work simplification is work measurement. Although designed primarily for production areas, it has had a moderate degree of success elsewhere, but the difficulty in establishing standards for paperwork has impeded the exploitation of its full potential.

The use of work simplification techniques can reduce costs and increase efficiency, and it is not the intent here to discredit the efficacy of this discipline. However, it must be said that these techniques were developed in the early 1900's, and, while the complexity and magnitude of industry and government have multiplied, the techniques of work simplification have remained relatively static. It is fairly evident that these techniques were designed for skirmishes and are not fully effective in waging total war. Had they been effective, the present condition would have been avoided. What is needed is a bold new approach to eliminate the tons rather than to scrape for the ounces.

WHY VALUE ENGINEERING?

Value engineering must be one of today's most misunderstood management techniques. It is variously termed value engineering, value analysis, and value control. Although the Value Engineering Council, the Electronics Industries Association, and the Society of American Value Engineers have judged these terms synonymous, there are constant attempts by practitioners and neophytes to assign different parameters to each.

To many managers, unfortunately, value engineering (the most widely used of the three terms) connotes an endeavor to make the already difficult job of managing more difficult by introducing a new glossary of technical terms. To the manager, value engineering belongs in the engineering department; how else account for the name? He remembers his last experiment in scientific management using integral calculus to determine his optimum staffing level and is now trying to comprehend the many variables involved in his latest computer feasibility study. He isn't looking for new management fads.

The term "value engineering" is really a misnomer, because it is not a strict analytical engineering discipline. It is described by Larry Miles, the "father of value engineering":

> . . . a philosophy implemented by the use of a specific set of techniques, a body of knowledge, and a group of learned skills. It is an organized creative approach which has for its purpose the efficient identification of unnecessary cost; that is, cost which provides neither quality nor use nor life nor appearance nor customer features.[1]

It is an attitude or philosophy, and the application of the specific set of techniques could be considered more an art than a science. However, in the formative years of value engineering, hardware seemed the most logical target. For maximum value, primary emphasis was therefore placed on promulgating the philosophy in engineering departments. Having attained a foothold there, the discipline took on the engineering identification.

The majority of value engineering techniques are not new, and their comprehension and application does not require an engineering degree. E. D. Heller describes the formation of the techniques:

> Most of the value engineering techniques are things which are familiar to all of us and, taken individually, are perhaps not to be

[1] Larry Miles, *Techniques of Value Analysis and Engineering*, McGraw-Hill Book Company, New York, 1961, p. 1.

considered new. The newness of value engineering lies in the use of all these techniques as a system. The systematic development of alternates to eliminate unnecessary costs is what makes value engineering effective. In other words, the elements of value engineering for the most part are not new; the newness lies in the system. The bricks may be used but the building is new.

However, certain of the value engineering techniques contain some new elements within them. These are the elements which deal with the approach to value through consideration of function.[2]

Larry Miles states, "Value engineering is not a substitute for conventional cost-reduction work methods. Rather, it is a potent and completely different procedure for accomplishing far greater results."[3] Since the paperwork and organization dilemma is now far greater than it was in the heyday of work simplification, it seems only axiomatic that a procedure for "accomplishing far greater results" be employed to resolve the dilemma.

Some advocates of value engineering abhor its use in anything but its pure state. To amalgamate it with techniques that are contained in an alien discipline is considered downright unprofessional. Others try to envelop value engineering in a series of mathematical formulas, while yet another faction views it strictly as a problem-solving device. However, reflection on these parochial views and the successful use of value engineering techniques in each only confirms the extreme flexibility and adaptability of value engineering itself. It *can* be used successfully in its pure state, assuming the pure state to be the techniques as first identified by Larry Miles. These techniques by their very nature prohibit a status quo condition. Subsequent chapters will show how value engineering techniques can even be amalgamated with the techniques of another discipline.

Value engineering techniques are needed in paperwork and organization, not because previous attempts to contain their enlargement have failed or because of prophecies of doom, but simply because their cost represents such a large portion of the total cost. The potential for savings in these areas is far in excess of that offered in

[2] E. D. Heller, "The Functional Technique," *Western Manufacturing*, December 1963.
[3] Miles, *loc. cit.*

hardware cost reduction. Most cost-reduction practices were originated specifically to reduce hardware costs. Companies now have value engineering departments, production engineering departments, manufacturing engineering departments, and motion study groups, all formed for the purpose of reducing *hardware* costs. Even the designer himself is more aware of and sensitive to cost in today's economy because many cost-reduction programs have come into being and because the cost-plus-fixed-fee contract era has been phasing out. Price has again gained predominance.

In contrast to hardware husbandry, the fertility of the paperwork and organization areas has seldom been attacked seriously. Periodically, government and industry survey results create renewed emphasis on reduction of paperwork and organization problems, but they seem to prosper in spite of these investigative efforts. Antiquated forms, superfluous information, unnecessary reports, and the nearly unlimited distribution of paper copies appear to enjoy a certain immunity in the American corporate system. Value analysis of management practices removes this immunity by providing principles and techniques to evaluate procedure and organization worth.

2

Value Analysis
of Management Practices

Value analysis of management practices is a unique combination of value engineering and work simplification techniques. It is designed to analyze and evaluate not only paperwork systems but also the organizations that produce the paperwork and was developed after an exhaustive review of work simplification practices and value engineering methods in use today. Its application can result in a synergistic increase in the value of an organization and its paperwork procedures.

When the huge potential reduction in paperwork cost became evident, programs were developed to clean out excessive paperwork and ineffective communication. As part of these programs, paperwork procedures were subjected to value engineering studies on the assumption that the techniques of value engineering could be applied to any project or endeavor. Since excellent results had been obtained in value engineering workshop seminars using hardware projects, the same degree of success was expected when paperwork projects were introduced. But the results were less than spectacular.

In analyzing a piece of hardware, the drawings, planning cards, cost data, and actual examples of the hardware were neatly packaged for each team. An apparently simple procedure, on the other hand, seemed to have a geometric growth factor proportional to the time spent in investigation. The seminar teams that were assigned to these projects noticeably lacked the enthusiasm displayed by the teams working on hardware. After only marginal success, the paperwork projects were abandoned—much to the relief of the instructor and his staff. The appraisal of these seminars was that the principles of value engineering could be used; the difficulty lay in finding something tangible enough to use them on. These techniques in their exact parameters could not fully contend with the expanse of paperwork projects.

At this point, little thought was given to the evaluation of an organization using value engineering. The feeling was that, if a simple paperwork procedure could foil the value engineer, the tentacles of an organizational project would certainly do so. Also, the interdependence of paperwork procedures and organization was not yet fully understood.

WORK SIMPLIFICATION

Other tools for cost reduction were reviewed for potential application. Although much has been written on the subject, only the techniques of work simplification appeared to have practical merit. Books and articles on work simplification were collected, training films were reviewed, and existing commercial seminar curriculums containing work simplification techniques were examined. Although work simplification lacked that certain flair of value engineering, it appeared to be the only answer; after all the data were collected, value engineers began to construct a work simplification workshop seminar.

Work simplification is a five-step pattern for attacking a problem and insuring a logical approach to developing a solution. At first glance, some of these steps seem to bear a striking resemblance to some value engineering techniques. The five steps are (1) selecting a job to improve, (2) getting all the facts, (3) challenging everything, (4) designing a new method, and (5) implementing the new method.

PROJECT SELECTION

The criteria used in selecting the jobs to improve—for example, bottleneck jobs, jobs that are time consuming, or high-scrap-rate jobs —can indicate high-cost areas; and the value engineering approach to project selection is usually parallel. Both disciplines attempt to get the most in cost reduction for the least amount of effort. For hardware, a glance at the accounting journals is often sufficient to identify a value engineering project, but the absence of adequate cost data on paper-work procedures in these same journals makes a more subjective or judgmental approach necessary. The many variables involved in selecting the proper procedure for study are treated in later chapters.

DATA COLLECTION

The edict to "get all the facts" has been tremendously over-worked in management courses, books, and articles. Getting all the facts will cost nothing but money, and it is analogous to obtaining maximum (rather than optimum) reliability. The ability to discriminate between the relevant and irrelevant facts in any study can significantly contribute to the success of the study. Conversely, the collection of irrelevant facts can muddy a situation beyond economic solution. If it were possible to collect all the facts germane to the situation, the future of business managers would be in serious jeopardy—for then the human faculty of judgment could be discarded as archaic and be replaced by the computer. If all pertinent facts were available, only one conclusion would be possible and there would therefore be no need to make a decision.

Although both disciplines advocate the collection of facts, work simplification offers the flow process chart, the multiple activity chart, the procedure flow chart, and the work distributor chart as specific tools for the collection of information. Displaying these charts on a wall can greatly facilitate their subsequent analysis and evaluation.

CHALLENGE EVERYTHING

Work simplification practitioners and value engineers both believe in challenging, but not exactly in the same sense. Value engineering uses the technique of challenging requirements, whereas work simplification challenges each detail in the step-by-step breakdown of the charted job. The steps that denote action are examined first on the premise that, if these "do" steps can be eliminated, the associated "make ready" and "put away" steps will automatically disappear. Each step is challenged by asking five questions:

1. What is done and why?
2. Where is it done and why?
3. When is it done and why?
4. Who does it and why?
5. How is it done and why?

The answers to these questions will usually result in simplification of a procedure by eliminating, combining, and resequencing steps. Upon completion of this interrogation a successful analysis is considered to have been conducted, and costs ordinarily are reduced.

The first major philosophical difference between work simplification and value engineering is found here. Work simplification reduces the cost of paperwork procedures, but it is basically a *systems-* or *product-oriented* study in which the parameters of the procedure being studied become the parameters of the study itself. The procedure is *assumed* to have value; thus the analysis usually results in retaining the same basic procedure with the frills removed. Because of the lack of a functional approach, the inherent danger of simplifying something that is totally unnecessary is always present. Work simplification doctors the *symptoms* of cost instead of analyzing the *cause* of the costs. This is a very important difference which stimulated considerable thought and ultimately led to the development of value analysis of management practices.

DEVELOPING AND IMPLEMENTING A NEW METHOD

The next step involves evaluating the suggested improvements on the basis of their probable success. Among the aspects that must be considered are the technical feasibility of putting the improvements into operation and the effect they will have on the safety and morale of employees. In addition, company procedures should be devised incorporating the potential improvements.

A degree of creative thinking is employed in this step, but it differs appreciably from the systematic and almost rigid application of creative thinking in the value engineering process where the output of the entire study depends on the emphasis and thoroughness exhibited at this stage in searching for alternative methods.

During the final stage of work simplification the principles of salesmanship, motivation by involvement, and reporting are used in much the same manner as in value engineering. The object is to sell. The techniques may have different names but they are essentially the same.

The proposal is installed experimentally to determine whether it is practicable under operating conditions. Revisions are made where necessary and a final report is prepared and published.

SUMMARY

An objective summary evaluation report on the techniques of work simplification used to reduce the cost of procedures and organizations cited three advantages:

1. The charting techniques provide an excellent vehicle to collect and display pertinent information.
2. The personnel involvement required in information collection is desirable.
3. The visualization afforded by wall charts is excellent.

In addition, six inadequacies were also noted:

1. The analysis of existing procedures lacks depth and substance.
2. It is a systems- or product-oriented study with output similar to input, only smaller.
3. No effort is made to determine essential function.
4. The development of alternative methods is extremely superficial.
5. The evaluation of alternatives lacks organization.
6. The danger of simplifying the unnecessary is ever present.

Work simplification stresses the charting and visualization of the existing procedures but glosses lightly over the analysis and evaluation. It does not provide alternative ways to accomplish the essential function of the procedure and therefore does not aim at maximum value. Although many concepts are similar, the methods of application differ substantially from value engineering practices.

VALUE ENGINEERING

Although it is not the intent of this book to explore fully all the value engineering tenets and techniques, an explanation of the basic concepts and most important techniques is essential to the understanding and application of VAMP. But, before treating the techniques of value engineering, the meaning of the word "value" should be considered.

MEASUREMENT OF VALUE

For more than 2,000 years, philosophers, economists, anthropologists, and sociologists have wrestled with the concept of value in an attempt to spell out a set of absolute conditions under which it could be measured and classified. Even Aristotle tried to define it. The progress since has been unspectacular, yet everyone seems to understand the term when it is used. Nevertheless, many theories have evolved through the centuries, each following its own axioms and excluding all others. The most popular of these were the utility theory, the labor theory, the cost theory, and the price theory of value.

The *utility theory* related the value of something to its utility—the more uses an item had the greater was its value. This theory was well liked by the early philosophers and appeared reasonable until someone reflected on the use of iron and the value of gold.

The *labor theory* of value proposed that labor and value are proportional—for example, native metal has no value until labor is expended to mine, transport, and refine it. If this were true, one could increase the value of a product simply by selecting the mode of production with the highest labor costs.

The *cost theory* equated cost with value and closely followed the labor theory, since all labor is cost. This can be rejected with the same reasoning used to refute the labor theory, for under this theory the value of a Christmas tree would be the same in June as it is in December.

The *price theory* argued that the price paid in exchange for an item is a measurement of its value. The inconsistency here is that if the value of the item to be traded were the same to the buyer and the seller, neither would be motivated and the exchange would never be executed.

From the preceding discussion, certain conclusions become evident:

1. Value is relative and is not an inherent feature of anything.
2. Value can be measured only by comparison.
3. Value is the relationship between what someone wants and what he is willing to give up in order to get it.

An examination of these conclusions reveals that the value of an item can be measured only by the individual desirous of attaining or retaining it.

TYPES OF VALUE

In value engineering, four categories are usually recognized as encompassing the total concept of value: use value, esteem or esthetic value, cost value, and exchange value.

1. *Use value* describes the power of an item to accomplish an end.
2. *Esteem* or *esthetic value* describes the feature or attractiveness of an item that causes it to be desired.
3. *Cost value* represents the effort that must be expended to acquire an item.
4. *Exchange value* is the quality of an item that allows trading the item for something else.

Most of the subsequent references to value will be restricted to use value, since its importance is paramount to paperwork procedures and organizations. For this purpose *maximum value* can be defined as the lowest possible cost to provide the essential function of a procedure or an organization.

VALUE ENGINEERING TECHNIQUES

The techniques that do not have major significance in paperwork procedures merit only a cursory treatment, while those that are germane to VAMP should be examined in greater depth.

1. *Job plan.* Value engineering is the use of specific techniques in an organized manner. This organization is provided by the job plan. Similar to the work simplification approach, the job plan comes in five steps or phases within which the remaining techniques are applied. One technique may have application peculiar to one specific phase while another may have application in all phases of the job plan. The five phases are (1) the information phase, (2) the creative phase, (3) the evaluation phase, (4) the investigation phase, and (5) the reporting phase.

The *information phase* consists of the gathering of information and the associated research connected with the study. For hardware this phase can be relatively well defined because drawings, unit cost data, planning procedures, and similar materials are usually available, but its application to paperwork can be seriously questioned. The industrial engineer may rightfully cite the lack of specific information-gathering techniques as the first and probably most flagrant value engineering deficiency in paperwork and organization application. It bolsters his original contention that value engineering was designed for hardware application only, and that's where it should stay. Yet the information phase can be considered the most important phase of the job plan, for an inadequate or superficial effort here restricts the efficacy of all other phases and may invalidate the entire study.

During the *creative phase*, imagination in the form of creative thinking is used to generate alternate methods of accomplishing the essential function of the item being studied. Each suggested alternate is recorded regardless of its apparent impracticability, and judgment of the recorded alternates is suspended. The technique of creative thinking was in existence before the advent of value engineering and is also used in work simplification. However, the manner in which this technique is used in value engineering differs greatly from its usage in work simplification, as will be explained later.

In the *evaluation phase* the suggested alternates are analyzed, not to eliminate alleged impractical ideas, but more in an effort to improve them to the point of acceptance. The ideas that have the greatest chance of success are selected for the next phase.

The *investigation phase* concerns the detailed development of the selected ideas, including the recognition of possible roadblocks to implementation. The preferred proposal is planned along with alternative proposals if feasible.

The *reporting phase* is a selling task, with all the pertinent data presented to those having the power to accept or reject the proposal. In value engineering it consists of a graphic presentation including before and after condition sketches with all pertinent cost data. If the previous phases have been adhered to and the other techniques have been used judiciously, the implementation of the proposal is almost certain.

2. *The functional approach.* This technique is the heart of value engineering and lends this discipline the unique character that distinguishes it from others. This approach uses a completely different reference point from other cost-reduction methods. It relates cost to function, whereas other disciplines relate cost to product.

The production engineer asks how a part can be made more cheaply; the value engineer asks how the function performed by the part can be provided at the least possible cost. If the item in question is an ash tray, production engineering might change the base material, the production methods, the quantity lots, and the tooling, but the resultant product would still be in the ash tray's basic configuration.

The value engineer would approach the same project by first determining the function that the ash tray performs. His study could result in the creation of ashless cigarettes with disintegrating filters.

To apply the functional approach fully, a series of questions must be asked and answered:

1. What is it?
2. What does it do?
3. What does it cost?
4. What is the function worth?
5. What else will accomplish the function?
6. What will that cost?

Answering the first question establishes parameters for the study. If the item to be studied is a component, and the study isn't restricted to that component but is enlarged to include many levels (subassembly, assembly, subsystem, system, and so forth), the study becomes so unwieldy that success is jeopardized. This does not preclude expansion of the study; it merely insures that any expansion is recognized as such and additional resources are obtained on that basis.

The answer to the second question provides functional definitions. This deceptively simple technique requires that each function of the item under study be defined with two words—a noun and a verb. This avoids the possibility of combining functions and at the same time insures that there will be a specific identification for each function. Such deliberation forces the value engineer to concentrate solely on the *function* rather than on the *characteristics* of the item. Selecting the proper function is extremely important because the entire creativity phase is based on the functional definition.

As an example, consider the refrigerator. What does it do? The first answer might be that it provides cold, and this is entered on the function definition worksheet (see Exhibit 1). However, this definition may not indicate the correct function, so further analysis is needed. To increase the abstraction, the question "Why does it do it?" is asked, and the answer that might be given is "preserves food." This definition is also entered on the worksheet. To the more specific question, "How does it do it?" the answer could be that it "transfers heat." This also is added to the list. After all the possible functional

Exhibit 1

FUNCTION DEFINITION WORKSHEET

COMPONENT	FUNCTION (VERB-NOUN)
refrigerator	~~provides~~ cold ~~transfers~~ heat preserves food

definitions are listed, the value engineer selects the one most pertinent to his study. Does he really want to *preserve food?* If so, he may gain better value by evaluating other methods, such as salting, smoking, radiation treatment, or canning. But if he actually wants to *provide cold,* he might then evaluate compression, servel refrigeration, cryogenic boil-off, and so on. Omitting this process could lead to selecting the incorrect function, and the subsequent evaluation would be of little value.

The next question—What does it cost?—refers to the total cost of the item being studied. In this case it would be the cost of the refrigerator itself.

The question, What is it worth? begins the evaluation phase. A product must have a *basic function* and one or more *secondary functions;* together they compose the *essential function.* The basic function is the purpose for which the item was designed. It is the reason for the item's existence and must remain even if everything else is eliminated. It is nearly always a *use* function. The value engineer with the refrigerator may decide that the basic function of his refrigerator is to provide cold. The secondary functions are features that exist because of the particular design approach taken to satisfy the basic function, such as making ice, chilling martinis, freezing steak, and storing eggs. These secondary functions are what the refrigerator does that makes it sell, gives it esteem value, or fulfills quality requirements. The functional evaluation is not finished until all the functions have been listed, identified as basic or secondary, and assigned a cost.

Ascertaining what it is worth provides the value engineer his yardstick to value. Previously it was shown that value is established only by comparison. Determining worth is essentially a matter of comparing similar functions. The secondary function provided by the special egg-storage rack can be compared to the lowest-cost way to store eggs in a refrigerator. This could well be the familiar sectioned cardboard egg container. Assuming that it cost approximately two cents, the function performed by the $8 or $10 built-in storage rack is worth only two cents in value. The difference between the $10 rack and the two-cent box can be expressed as *esteem* value.

A comparison of the function's actual cost and its worth will give an estimated measured value for the function. Value relationships have often been expressed mathematically by the formula:

$$V_{max} = \frac{F}{C_{min}}$$

in which V = value, F = function, and C = cost.

The functional approach differs considerably from the work simplification technique in that it establishes optimum, measurable study objectives. Instead of saying, "This item costs *too* much," after a functional evaluation the analyst can say, "The cost of this item is x and its use value is y. The objective of the study will be to reduce the item cost as close to y as we can."

The creative thinking phase of the job plan is entered into by asking "what else will accomplish the function." After attention is fixed on the function of the item rather than on the item itself, the search for alternate methods is initiated. A team approach will increase the number of suggestions, and every effort should be made to draw ideas from individuals with varied backgrounds. All judgment concerning the merit of each idea is suspended.

Every idea, no matter how ludicrous it may seem, should be recorded on a blackboard or some other visual aid so as to stimulate other ideas. The team members must be encouraged to come up with novel and unorthodox suggestions, for these are the type that often contribute most to the success of the study. When all possible alternates have been listed, each idea is then reviewed for merit. The ideas that best perform the function and have the highest degree of acceptance and possibility for implementation are selected and the question—What will that cost?—is applied to them. The assignment of estimated costs will usually refine the possibilities to a few ideas and establish priorities for these few. Then the best of these are selected for futher development and eventual installation. At this point, the functional approach is complete.

3. *Blast-create-refine.* The blast-create-refine technique is one that partially incorporates the functional approach and is extremely important in evaluating paperwork procedures. It is based on the premise that it is far more effective to begin with a simple concept, analyze it, and add only those costs deemed necessary than it is to evaluate a complex procedure or item and identify and remove those areas containing unnecessary costs.

The *blast* phase requires the identification of the basic functions only, temporarily disregarding all secondary functions. The *create* phase involves the development of alternate methods to accomplish the basic functions revealed during the blast phase, and at the lowest possible cost. These methods are then *refined* by adding or revising to the point where they become satisfactory. As each secondary function is reviewed, additional revisions will be necessary and the refinement continues until the essential function of the procedure or item has been provided. At this point, maximum potential value is attained.

4. *Roadblocks to change.* Niccolò Machiavelli was not the first to recognize the almost natural reluctance of people to submit to change, but he did express it quite succinctly in *The Prince* when he wrote:

It must be considered that there is nothing more difficult to carry out, nor more doubtful of success, nor more dangerous to handle, than to initiate a new order of things. For the reformer has enemies in all those who profit by the old order, and only lukewarm defenders in all those who would profit by the new order, this lukewarmness arising partly from fear of their adversaries, who have the law in their favour; and partly from the incredulity of mankind, who do not truly believe in anything new until they have had the actual experience of it.

Resistance to change is grounded in attitudes and habits that are difficult to overcome. Since attitudes and habits form opinions, and since opinions govern actions, negative attitudes will produce negative actions—roadblocks to progress.

There are numerous reasons for resistance to change, and the roadblocks that result from this resistance take many forms. Personal prejudice has proved to be an effective block against the implementation of many good ideas. An idea may be good but the "wrong" person suggested it. The excuses used by the manager for ignoring the merit of the idea are all too familiar:

- He's a troublemaker—always coming up with divergent ideas. His solution is too radical, too different to be any good.
- He just doesn't understand the problem. It is far too complicated for such a simple solution. If it were that easy, I'd have thought of it.
- He thinks he's a mechanical genius, but we tried that ten years ago. Besides, I've been in this business for twenty years and he's been around for only two.
- He's a smart aleck with a wise remark for everything. He's always running off at the mouth, and he's much too shallow to have a good idea.
- He doesn't even have a degree; he couldn't possibly be creative. *I've* got a master's degree and *he* has the gall to suggest a solution.
- He's been after my job for months and I'm not going to back up his suggestion.

Certain phrases can also indicate a potential roadblock: We don't have time. Don't argue with success. We can't afford it. Our company is different. It's against company policy. It's been done this way for years; why change now? All these can identify the first step in constructing a roadblock. They must be anticipated and then specifically defined as clearly and as sharply as possible. Once defined, plans to overcome them can be formulated.

It is generally agreed that for the most part people dislike change and will resist new ideas and new ways of doing things. However, this is not always true. People may welcome change if they believe that (1) they are the initiators rather than mere recipients of the change, (2) they have something to gain from the change, or (3) they have nothing to lose as a result of the change.

Value engineering is directed toward stimulating change by developing an attitude of constructive discontent with poor value. Good human relations holds the key. When people are treated with dignity and respect, good rapport can be established and maintained by the value engineer. This lead-in, coupled with the concepts of participation and involvement and the absence of critical negativism, can overcome many roadblocks. The use of good human relations will make others a part of the effort to achieve better value. In value engineering, an awareness of the fears and anxieties that trouble people coupled with a large amount of empathy is the way to attain success.

5. *Challenging requirements.* One of the most significant reasons for poor value is the establishment of a procedure to provide for temporary deviations from the norm. Although the temporary conditions eventually pass, the procedure often has an enviable longevity. Written procedures seem to enjoy a special exemption from criticism, and to challenge them is considered tantamount to idiocy. Yet successful application of both value engineering and work simplification requires that procedures be challenged for several reasons:

- The dynamic nature of science and the economy renders many of yesterday's requirements and specifications obsolete.
- Lack of proper communication can establish unnecessary requirements.
- Original requirements may have been hastily established because of insufficient time to evaluate alternatives.
- Many times fringe requirements are established because of an ignorance of cost data. Thousands of examples can be seen in the form of drawing tolerances.

It should be noted that requirements have value only when they are used to obtain the functions desired by the user; undesired functions have *no* value.

6. *Other value engineering techniques.* That the remaining common techniques are grouped into one short paragraph without detailed explanations in no way denies their importance and value in pursuing hardware studies; it indicates only that their efficiency in paperwork projects is evident or has yet to be demonstrated. They are included here merely to round out this basic overview of value engineering.

- Use information from only the best source.
- Analyze costs.
- Use specialty vendors.
- Use the company's specialists.
- Use standards.
- Get new information.
- Get a dollar sign on everything.
- Work on specifics—avoid generalities.
- Use your own judgment.
- Use the criterion, "Would I spend my money this way?"

These techniques together with those itemized earlier do not constitute value engineering in its entirety. Other facets such as value standards, cost target programs, and value trade-offs have considerable merit in hardware application. Since their application to paperwork is minimal and since a cursory explanation would be inadequate for understanding and use, these topics have been left to a detailed study of value engineering.

Value engineering contains inherent characteristics that preclude a status quo condition, and, as the discipline develops, new uses and techniques will undoubtedly be uncovered and assimilated.

SUMMARY

An objective review of the advantages and deficiencies of both disciplines in treating the paperwork dilemma quickly reveals several complementary features (see Exhibit 2).

Although each is useful in reducing costs in specific areas, neither is sufficiently flexible to allow complete application throughout the maze of paperwork procedures. The philosophies differ. Work sim-

Exhibit 2

WORK SIMPLIFICATION AND VALUE ENGINEERING: A COMPARISON

MAJOR ADVANTAGES

Work Simplification	Value Engineering
Provides investigative tools	Is function-oriented
Uses visualization	Uses functional evaluation
	Develops alternative methods

MAJOR DEFICIENCIES

Is systems-oriented	Lacks visualization
Provides no alternatives	Employs no investigative tools
Sets no value parameters	

plification reduces the cost of paperwork by eliminating, combining, and resequencing operations without much analysis of the purpose of the procedure. Value engineering reduces the cost of an item by analyzing its purpose and developing other methods to accomplish the selected function at the lowest possible price. Work simplification provides investigative techniques and important visualization aspects lacking in the paperwork application of value engineering. The most important technique of work simplification is the visualization—the wall-chart portrayal of an existing procedure. If this technique could be combined with the functional approach of value engineering, a synergistic result would be obtained.

3

Integration of Techniques

To avoid repeating action already devised for integrating work simplification and value engineering techniques, a survey was made of companies noted for their leadership in work simplification use and training. In addition, the proceedings of several conferences and the contents of professional journals were researched for the same reason. The survey revealed that some companies which claimed to have accomplished the integration had merely combined the two techniques without really integrating them. For example, to existing manuals on work simplification they had just added another chapter on value engineering. The articles appearing in professional journals on paperwork reduction sometimes alluded to the use of value engineering techniques, but the integration of techniques was never mentioned. And the suggestions for using value engineering never really explained how to do it. Thus the basic idea of using value engineering to reduce paperwork costs cannot be said to originate with VAMP. What *is* new is the development of a set of techniques to allow application of value engineering to the solution of the problem.

Initially the integration of work simplification and value engineering techniques concerned only the reduction of paperwork procedures, and the flow process chart and the multicolumn procedure chart were selected from work simplification as the most apt tools for adaptation to VAMP. These two charts were expected to provide a base line or a starting block for the subsequent functional evaluation process.

FLOW PROCESS CHART

The flow process chart shown in Exhibit 3 has long been a mainstay of work simplification. It is used as an aid in finding a better way to do a job by portraying graphically, in sequence, the steps taken by an individual or a piece of material to perform a task. Usually the chart is prepared by an industrial engineer who actually

Exhibit 3

FLOW PROCESS CHART

SUMMARY							NO. 435 PAGE 1 OF 5

JOB EMPLOYEE SUGGESTION FORM

☐ MAN OR [X] MATERIAL _____
CHART BEGINS RECEIPT OF FORM
CHART ENDS FILING OF FORM
CHARTED BY E. A. L. DATE 3/15/8

#	DETAILS OF (PRESENT/PROPOSED) METHOD	OPERATION / TRANSPORT / INSPECTION / DELAY / STORAGE	DISTANCE IN FEET	QUANTITY	TIME	ANALYSIS (WHAT? WHERE? WHEN? WHO? HOW? WHY?)	NOTES	ACTION
1	OPEN ENVELOPE	○⇨☐D▽	–	150	.5			
2	REMOVE FORM	○⇨☐D▽	–	150	.1			
3	DATE STAMP	○⇨☐D▽	–	150	.8			
4	LEADMAN	○⇨☐D▽	20	150	1.0			
5	REVIEW FORM	○⇨☐D▽	–	150	2.0			
6	ASSIGN ANALYST	○⇨☐D▽	–	150	2.0			
7	CLERK	○⇨☐D▽	20	150	1.0			
8	SERIALIZE FORM	○⇨☐D▽	–	150	.8			
9	RECORD IN RECEIPT LOG	○⇨☐D▽	–	150	1.5			

follows the man or material through the task as it is being performed. Each element of the task is identified sequentially by a flow line from one symbol to another. These symbols represent the type of action being performed and are important in identifying the *do* or costly elements of the task. (See Exhibit 4.) The time it takes to complete each element is recorded and summarized, and the total time becomes the base line on which to measure the success of the study.

When the existing method has been completely charted, the industrial engineer reviews each element by mentally asking himself the following questions:

- Why is it being done?
- Why is it being done here?
- Why is it being done at this time?
- Why is it being done by this person?
- Why is it being done in this manner?

The answers to these questions will often stimulate the analyst to eliminate, combine, or resequence the elements for greater efficiency. After the review and analysis, the industrial engineer prepares another flow process chart incorporating his proposed improvements and completes the summary block on the top of the form. The time differences in each type of element (assuming a reduction from the existing method) become the basis for claimed savings.

For adaptation to VAMP, certain modifications were incorporated to permit the use of the functional approach and to identify element costs more clearly. The VAMP flow process chart is prepared in basically the same manner as the chart described earlier except that a cost column has been added next to the time column.

Elapsed time does not always represent cost expenditure. Delay time costs nothing when it does not affect a schedule, and the reduction of this delay time by 50 percent cannot logically serve as the basis for a saving. Likewise, storage time may realistically involve no added expenditures when unused storage space is available. And transportation time cannot represent real cost when the vehicle of transit is constant. For these reasons, the elapsed time of each element is translated into actual cost. Upon chart completion, the element costs become the analysis priorities.

The other significant change in the format is the provision for

Exhibit 4

PROCEDURE FLOW CHART SYMBOLS

◯	OPERATION	Indicates an event denoting "work" or change
◎	CREATE	Indicates the origin of a new form, record, and so forth
◍	ADD	Indicates something added to a form or record, such as signing, posting, or stamping
▷	TRANSPORT	Indicates moving something from one place to another
D	DELAY	Indicates a planned or unplanned temporary delay
☐	INSPECT	Indicates an examination or verification such as a signature authorization
◇	DECIDE	Indicates choosing a course of action from alternates
▽	STORE	Indicates retaining something for future use or reference
▽	DISCARD	Indicates eliminating something from the procedure

functional definitions in the description of the task elements. During analysis, the highest-cost operation element is selected first and a functional definition is assigned. Alternate methods of accomplishing the element are developed by the analyst and the most cost-effective one is selected for the proposed method. The next costly operation element is then subjected to the same procedure, and so on until all of them have been analyzed. Time permitting, the other costly elements are analyzed in the same manner. When the analysis has been finished, a proposed flow process chart is prepared and the summary at the top of the form is completed. The net cost difference and the expression of this difference as a percentage of total cost are extremely helpful in overcoming roadblocks to the implementation of proposed changes.

The use of the flow process chart can be overdone. Indiscriminate and detailed use will severely diminish the ratio of saving to cost. The task selected for this study *must* be of sufficient cost magnitude to justify the expense of the study, and the element definitions should encompass a reasonable cost package. There is a tendency in using this chart to define the elements in abundant detail, which increases study cost and minimizes potential savings. Because of its simple logical approach, the flow process chart has been used with beneficial results in training seminars as a lead into procedure flow charting. It is also useful in further defining a high-cost area that has been identified but not detailed in a procedure flow chart.

Procedure Flow Chart

There are probably as many ways to prepare a procedure flow chart as there are procedures to be charted. The popular multicolumn flow chart (Exhibit 5) is used primarily to visualize the processing of a multipage form. The horizontal flow chart (Exhibit 6) is designed to portray the relationship of paperwork to operations. There is also a vertical flow chart and most likely someone, somewhere, has designed one on the bias. The variations of each of the basic chart directions (time-phased, sequential, department-oriented, and the rest) are too numerous to describe here. The point is that no method of procedure flow charting has been universally accepted as the one "right" way, to the exclusion of all others. Each has merit, depending upon the circumstances and function of the chart. A flow chart to explain a written procedure may be completely different from one used to supplement an oral presentation.

The horizontal procedure flow chart was selected for VAMP because it permits the widest latitude of visualization and has the flexibility to portray a procedure of any size. Where the flow process chart is restricted to describing the task of *one* individual or *one* piece of material at a time, the procedure flow chart can visualize the interaction of many individuals with many pieces of material and can provide a specific base line for the application of value engineering techniques. It represents where we are now and is analogous to having the hardware present during a typical value engineering study. (The preparation of the procedure flow chart is explained in detail in Chapter 8.)

Exhibit 5

PROCEDURE FLOW CHART: TUITION REFUND

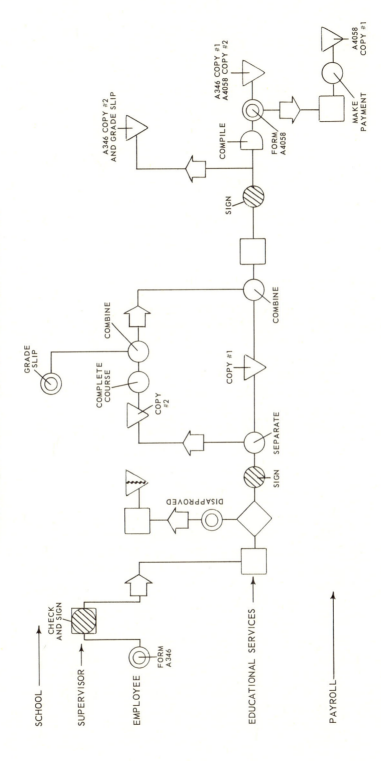

Exhibit 6

HORIZONTAL PROCEDURE FLOW CHART:
INCOME TAX RETURN

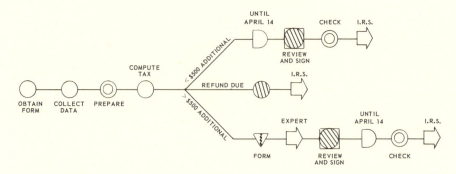

The blast-create-refine technique is applied to the completed procedure flow chart by identifying first the basic function or functions of the procedure and then the secondary functions and circling them in red on the wall chart. (See Exhibit 7.) A variety of methods for accomplishing the basic function are developed, and, after selecting the best of these, the remaining secondary functions are analyzed in the same manner and refined by adding only those elements that are required. The proposed new method is then charted for use during the implementation phase.

ORGANIZATION

In determining the basic functions of a procedure, it is necessary in many cases to examine the organization responsible for originating the procedure. These unscientific explorations into organization per se were what prompted the search for some means by which the functions of the organization could be determined and evaluated. It became evident that organization value analysis must logically precede any attempt to analyze the value of the procedural output of the organization, and VAMP was forced to expand its scope to include the concept of organization. With investigative or data-collection tools lacking, value engineering again dipped into the work simplification vault for assistance.

The work distribution chart in Exhibit 8 was reviewed for possible adoption. The purpose of the chart is to identify to the manager

Exhibit 7

PROCESSING A DISCREPANCY REPORT

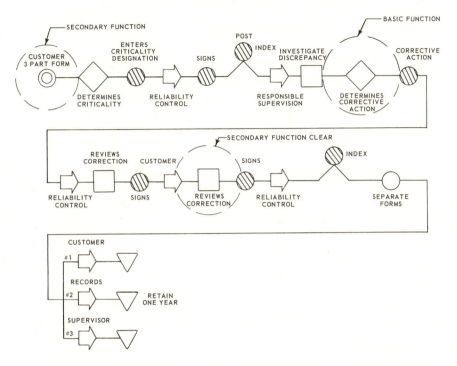

the type or nature of the work being done by his organization, to identify the individuals doing the work, and to determine the quantity of work being performed. The objective of the overall study is work improvement through the proper use of available skills and the provision of a balanced workload.

To develop the work distribution chart requires several supporting forms—an activity list, individual task data lists, and summary task lists. The activity list, which is prepared by the manager, enumerates in order of importance all the activities that the organization performs. The task data sheets are prepared daily by every employee during the survey period. They list the different tasks each employee performs, the number of times he performs each task, and the total time spent on each. At the end of the survey the manager collects the task data lists, summarizes the information on them, and prepares one task list for each employee. The work distribution chart is then made, using the data from the activity list and the task lists.

Exhibit 8

WORK DISTRIBUTION CHART

STEP 1 — VERTICALLY SCAN ACTIVITY COLUMN (WHY, WHAT) (NECESSITY, FUNCTION, HOURS SPENT)

STEP 2 — HORIZONTALLY SCAN EACH ACTIVITY (WHERE, WHEN, WHO) (SPECIALIZATION, FLEXIBILITY, BOTTLENECKS, DUPLICATION, BATCHING, COMBINING)

STEP 3 — VERTICALLY SCAN EACH PERSON (HOW) (RELATED TASKS, SKILLS, DEADLINE WORK, WORKLOAD)

ORGANIZATIONAL UNIT CHARTED: Credit & Collection			NAME: J. Brown		NAME: H. Black		NAME: R. Green		NAME: K. White		NAME: M. Blue		NAME: J. Jones		NAME: M. Schwartz	
EXISTING ORGANIZATION X / RECOMMENDED ORGANIZATION		DATE 4/26/61	POSITION Supervisor		POSITION Clerk		POSITION Coll.Cont. Clerk		POSITION Coll. Cont. Clerk		POSITION Coll. Chkg. Clerk		POSITION Coll. Chkg. Clerk		POSITION Mail Clerk	
CHARTED BY J. Brown		APPROVED BY J. King	GRADE Section		GRADE Senior		GRADE Utility		GRADE Utility		GRADE General		GRADE General		GRADE Service	
ACTIVITY NUMBER	ACTIVITY (FUNCTION)	HOURS PER WEEK	TASKS	HOURS PER WEEK	TASKS	HOURS PER WEEK	TASKS *Reduce by New Coding*	HOURS PER WEEK	TASKS *Combine Activity*	HOURS PER WEEK	TASKS *Transfer to other Dept.*	HOURS PER WEEK	TASKS *Reduce Information on List*	HOURS PER WEEK	TASKS	HOURS PER WEEK
1.	Collection, Current Accounts	63	Investigate Paymt.	1	Current Acct Review	5	Process Notices	7	Maint. Ind. Acc'ts	4	Prepare Fld. List	1¼				
					Transfer to lower Grade Clerk		Process M.U.A.s	3½	" Mds.	3	Filing & Check'g.	2				
							Arrange M.U.A.s for Field	6½	Prepare Lancaster Collection Route	5	Check'g Payments	4				
					Eliminate by Increasing		Review Field Work	6	Review Lancaster Field Work	1¼						
			Misdirected Effort		*Min. to $50*		Activity on Returned Checks	1	Investigate Paymt.	12½	*Mostly Duplication*					
2.	Collection, Closed Accounts	60¼	Review Incom. Mail	1¾	Cl. Acct Reviews	12½	Phone Inquiries	5½	Post Payments to B.D.s	1¾	Process Closing Bill Notices	8¾	*Change Time Sequence to Eliminate 90%*			
			Investigate Paymt.	3	Dictate Letters	5	*Wrong Dept.!*		Process Agency Accounts	¾	Process Trial Balance List	6				
			Transfer to lower Grade		*Clerk*				Investigate Transfer & B.D.s	3¼	Process Bad Debt List	2				
											Prepare Cards for Collection Agency	1½				
											Checking Acc'ts.	6½	*Excessive. Try sampling*			
											Proposal to Transfer	2				
3.	Bill Distribution	51½			*Screen to*						Returned Mail	¾	Returned Mail	¾	Bill Processing (Manually)	37½
	Centralize for Mechanization		*Sales Dept. Function?*		*Reduce Volume*								Operate Inserting & Postal Machines	12½	*Centralize for mechanized Billing*	
4.	Credit	29¼	App. Appliance Sales	1½	Review NonRes Cred	5	Phone Inquiries	6	*Request Phone Co. Survey*				Chkg. Deposit T.C.	10	*No Value Eliminate*	
			Dictate Cr. Letters	5	*Use more*								Review Deposit(Field)	¼		
			App. Cred. NonRes.	1¾	*Form Letters*											
5.	Administration & Training	31¼	Daily Att. Reports	½	Lead Clerk	5										
			Supervision	15												
			Meetings	1¾												
			Wk. Simplification	3	Job Training	5					*Not our Function Transfer to Proper Dept.*					
	Check if all OUR Function		Quality Control	1			*Supervisory Control?*									
6.	Miscellaneous	27¼	Inter & Miscel.	2¼			Stationery Requis. and Inventory	2	Process Mail Paymt.	2½	Ret. Contingency Fund Memos.	¾	Door Box Payments	6½		
									Miscel. Typing	2¼	Miscel.	2	Miscel.	7½		
									Miscel. Interup.	1¼	*Transfer to Lower Grade Clerk*					
SUBTOTALS OR TOTALS (MAN-HOURS)		262½		37½		37½		37½		37½		37½		37½		37½

The analysis of the work distribution chart is usually conducted in three separate phases. The activities listed in the first column are reviewed and analyzed in what is called the *organizational view*. Do the activities really reflect the purpose of the organization? Does each activity logically belong in this particular organization? Can the activity be performed elsewhere more economically? The answers to these and other questions complete the organizational view.

After any proposed changes are recorded, the next phase begins. The second step reviews and analyzes the tasks associated with each activity. The same type of questioning used in the organizational view is used in this *departmental view*. Does the task support the associated activity? Are tasks being duplicated? Should the task be done in this way at this time? This view often results in the identification and subsequent elimination of redundant tasks.

The proposed changes are recorded and the third phase, *the personal view*, is initiated. In this view the manager reviews the tasks performed by each individual in an attempt to upgrade the employee and downgrade the tasks he performs. Ideally, monotonous jobs are made interesting, workload is adjusted equitably, and all individuals are given the opportunity to express their creative urge. When the actions necessary to attain these goals are developed, the analysis is complete and a new wall chart is prepared.

The value engineering evaluation of the work distribution chart resulted in the immediate adoption of the basic techniques for collecting the data. In addition, it provided visibility in a wall chart and almost dictated diagnosis, prognosis, and treatment. The only notable lack was the method of analysis. Usually the first question asked in the analysis of the work distribution chart is whether the activities listed really reflect the purpose of the organization. However, no overt attempt is made prior to the analysis to determine and define the purpose of the organization. Without a definition of the basic and secondary functions of the organization, the answers to any of the common analytical questions are really meaningless. Thus a method that would provide a functional approach had to be developed.

The analysis of activities provided by a work distribution study also lacked depth. The accepted vernacular to describe the activities of an organization (determine policy, maintain program control, coordinate manufacturing problems) is much too abstract to tolerate an analytical examination. The widespread and popular use of management jargon can often be attributed to the manager's very sketchy understanding of exactly what tasks should be performed to accomplish his organization's prime objectives, since these objectives have seldom been clearly defined to him. It became obvious that the organization's activities as well as the organization itself would have to be reduced to functional definitions for any serious analysis.

ORGANIZATION VALUE ANALYSIS

Organization value analysis was developed to supply a set of techniques and a procedure for their application in order to maximize the value of an organization. It is, in essence, the functional approach applied to the work distribution chart. The heart of organization value analysis is the organization value analysis chart, shown in Exhibit 9, which is basically the work distribution chart modified. The name was changed to describe its function more accurately. Its purpose is not to distribute work but to describe the work being performed in terms sufficient for functional analysis. The data are collected using the same supporting forms as those used with the work distribution chart, and in general the same procedure is followed in preparing OVAC. The analysis of the completed chart, however, takes on a completely new light.

The OVAC analysis begins with defining the basic and secondary function of the organization being studied and recording these functions on the chart. The importance of this step cannot be overemphasized, for a shallow or cursory treatment here will seriously affect the entire analysis. There is a natural tendency for the analyst to pass lightly over this phase, and as a result it is often only the most obvious functions that are listed. For example, the basic function of the program control department is most likely to be defined with the words, "control program," and the weights analysis department's basic function becomes "analyze weight." Superficial examinations such as these may render all subsequent analysis fruitless, for the entire study depends on an accurate definition. If "analyze weight" is selected, then any activity or task of the organization that contributes to the analysis of weights will probably be adjudged necessary and valuable. However, if the basic function is determined to be "reduce weight," a completely different set of circumstances and conditions

Exhibit 9

ORGANIZATION VALUE ANALYSIS CHART

FUNCTIONS
BASIC (VERB-NOUN): Assure Accuracy
SECONDARY (VERB-NOUN):

ORGANIZATIONAL UNIT CHARTED: CALIBRATION LABORATORY
DATE:
PRESENT ORGANIZATION: ✓
PROPOSED ORGANIZATION:

CHARTED BY:
APPROVED BY:

#	ACTIVITY (VERB-NOUN)	HRS. PER WEEK	COST PER WEEK	% OF TOTAL	A. E. Little — Supervisor — TASKS (INDIVIDUAL)	HRS.	J. Brown — Calibration Engineer — TASKS (INDIVIDUAL)	HRS.	R. Frazer — Calibration Technician — TASKS (INDIVIDUAL)	HRS.	J. Thomas — Calibration Technician — TASKS (INDIVIDUAL)	HRS.	L. Smith — Calibration Technician — TASKS (INDIVIDUAL)	HRS.
1	Calibrate Equipment	45	270	22			Approve Calibration	6	Set up Equipment	6	Read Manual	1	Confer with User	2
									Reduce Data		Set up Equipment	1	Read Manual	1
									Calibrate Equipment	6	Calibrate Equipment	10	Calibrate Equipment	7
									Record Calibration	2	Record Calibration	2	Record Calibration	5
2	Trouble-Shoot and Repair	22	132	11			Assist Technicians	12	Confer with User	3	Confer with User	1		
									Determine Trouble	5				
									Repair Equipment	1				
3	Control Equipment	56	336	27	Prepare Reports	4	Establish Calibration Intervals	4	Pick up and Deliver ✗	12	Pick up and Deliver ✗	15	Pick up and Deliver ✗	19
					Establish Priorities	2								
4	Procure Equipment ✗	28	168	14	Consult User	4	Review Equipment Available and Select ✗	4	Order Repair Parts ✗	10	Pick up Repair Parts ✗	7	Order Repair Parts ✗	3
5	Provide Technical Information	30	180	15	Meetings	22	Technical Liaison Meetings	8						
6	Miscellaneous	21	126	11	Supervise and Administer	10			Meetings	2	Meetings	3	Clean up	3
									Clean up	3				
	TOTAL	202	1212	100		42		40		40		40		40

will prevail. Perhaps the basic function could even be satisfied without analysis—by a new process offering real cost advantages.

Once the essential function of the organization is defined and
recorded, it is subjected to the creativity phase of value engineering.
Various other possibilities for accomplishing the basic function are
developed and recorded, with judgment suspended until all have been
listed. Each alternate is then reviewed and those that warrant further
investigation are recorded on an OVAC activity/task analysis sheet,
as illustrated in Exhibit 10. Additional refinement by introducing cost
data and other variables should result in the final selection of the one
best method of fulfilling the function. One or two alternates to the
best method should also be listed in case the selected method cannot
be implemented.

ACTIVITY/TASK ANALYSIS SHEET & ALTERNATE FUNCTIONS

ACTIVITY NO. _____3_____   COST PER WEEK $ ___336___

_____Control Equipment_____

ALTERNATES

1	Customer Deliver & Pick-up
2	Mobile Calibration Teams
3	In-place Calibrations
4	Existing Transportation Facilities
5	
6	
7	

SELECTION		EST. COST
1	Existing Transportation Facilities	$ 20 / wk
2	In-place Calibration	195 / wk
3	Customer Deliver & Pick-up	240 / wk

Exhibit 10

If the creative phase dictates an entirely new concept necessitating a drastic revision of the existing organization, the analysis of the organization ceases. Necessary activities and tasks are added to the basic function until the function is workable. Staffing is developed on the basis of the tasks and a new OVAC wall chart is prepared.

In instances where no drastic innovation is proposed, the analysis continues. Each listed activity beginning with the most expensive is reduced to a functional definition. The activity "coordinate engineering aspects," which really consists of instructing neighboring departments on how to do their jobs, is translated by the functional definition into "teach employees." Again, considerable care must be exercised to insure that the functional definition selected is really the one that best explains the activity in specific concrete words.

The function defined for the first activity is compared to the primary and secondary functions of the organization recorded on the top of the chart. It is necessary to determine whether the activity directly supports the essential function of the organization. If it is not required, the entire activity with its associated tasks should be eliminated. When an activity *is* found to contribute to the organization's essential function, the creative phase is initiated in the same manner as that used on the functional definition of the organization.

After the OVAC analysis sheet is prepared and the best method is selected, the proposed activity is used on the new chart. When all activities—or at least the most expensive ones—have been analyzed, the high-cost tasks are reviewed by evaluating their need in light of the functional definition of the activity they support: Can the function be performed without this task?

Upon completion of the analysis, a new OVAC is prepared incorporating the proposed changes. This new OVAC, when compared to the chart of the existing organization, can often hasten implementation of the proposed organization. However, the degree of difference displayed is dependent upon the degree of objectivity used by the analyzers.

4

Selecting
an Organization for Study

THE "organization" has been under fire from every quarter and has been accused of crimes ranging from moral turpitude to treason. It is ridiculed by philosophers and psychologists, condemned by professors, and adored by stockholders. It has transformed authors into business experts overnight as well as providing them with topics for many fictional best sellers. Indeed, some of this fiction is used as business college course material and is accorded the same degree of respect and validity as an accounting text.

Like religion, the word "organization" can quickly evoke controversy. It has a number of definitions, and there are many types. But it has one common element—the collaboration of two or more *people* to attain some objective unattainable by the individual alone.

Since *people* are the essence of organization, organization value analysis must be deeply concerned with people. "Man is a political animal," said Aristotle, and this aspect of man's nature demands special consideration. Man also has certain needs which are normally expressed from the highest to the lowest as creative, ego, social, safety, and physiological. As the lowest need is satisfied, the next higher need comes to the fore. The appeal to man's creative need, the highest in order of normal attainment, will develop only when all the lower needs have been satisfied to some degree.

The creative need and in part the ego need that are appealed to in organization value analysis cannot be aroused if the safety need is jeopardized. Man will not fashion the club with which he is to be beaten, and it is ludicrous to expect automatic and enthusiastic cooperation from employees who know that their participation in a study may remove the source of their bread. But to conduct a study without the active cooperation of the employees will result in limited success and may create significant morale problems, not only in the organization being studied, but also in any neighboring organization.

Much of the literature concerning the work distribution chart and its analysis is laced with an air of naïveté or fantasy. Employees are always upgraded and jobs are always downgraded. Everyone wins and the expression "termination of employment" is never used, nor is its existence admitted. Unfortunately, this gets a bit sticky in real life when costs have to be reduced because of economic retrenchment. Even the most sincere humanitarian will agree that under particular business conditions, layoffs are inevitable if the company is to survive. Organizational value analysis *can* be used beneficially in such cases after experience has been gained in its use, but the method of application differs radically from the standard.

The work distribution chart, it is said, can be used with an organization of any size and nature, and organization value analysis makes the same claim. But if a measurable degree of success is desired, certain restrictions become apparent and selecting the "right" organization for study becomes an important consideration in guaranteeing tangible and profitable results.

Since organization value analysis is a systematic creative method for optimizing the value of an organization, it should be applied from the top down for maximum profit. Although this theory is quite logical, the company president may not always agree that his office is the best place to start. A degree of resistance will be encountered at any level of organization, but the degree can be minimized by motivating the organization's supervisor to *want* to participate in the study. Conversely, the resistance can be maximized by directing or demanding that the organization's supervisor accede to the study.

Organization value analysis is based on the precept that the person most qualified to analyze a specific organizational element is the supervisor of the group to be studied. Organization consultants can be employed to analyze the organization, but their source of information basically is the group supervisor. Of course, the supervisor will relate to the consultant only the data that will reflect favorably on him. Although the consultant may not base his analysis entirely on the data he receives in this manner and may use industrial factoring, his grasp of the overall situation will be less than desired because of the unrevealed information. In an ordered study of a particular organization, the criticism implicit in the demand will establish supervisory roadblocks that are difficult to overcome. For these reasons, the supervisor's cooperation and sincere desire to improve his group must be assured prior to a study. This assurance can best be attained by selecting an organization where the supervisor has nothing to lose and something to gain by the study. There has to be "something in it for him."

CRITERIA FOR SELECTION

The conditions under which organization value analysis can flourish will vary from company to company and from industry to industry, depending upon the type of leadership and the organizational habits. There are, however, broad selective criteria that will generally minimize friction and insure acceptance.

The new supervisor. A newly assigned supervisor is particularly receptive to the tenets of organization value analysis. He is probably fresh from a seminar in management principles and sufficiently open-minded to at least listen to a proposal on the subject. He is likely to be energetic and enthusiastic and to avail himself of any management techniques that will increase his professionalism and assist him in his climb to higher management. He can see that a study of this nature will allow him to examine each facet of his new organization overtly and gain insight into the organization that otherwise would take months of tactful questioning.

Above all, the new supervisor's appraisal of proposed improvements can be conducted with the objectivity of one whose authorship is not being questioned, since the original organization was established prior to his appointment. The newly assigned supervisor does not imperil himself in any way by participating in an organization value analysis study of his group.

The reassigned supervisor. A supervisor recently assigned to direct a new organization is a source of study potential. He is normally faced with the challenge of improving the efficiency of his new charges, and, if this challenge is not an explicit requirement of his new assignment, the supervisor will establish a self-imposed objective of improvement. His new assignment creates a condition where his managerial skills can be easily measured by his superiors simply by comparing the results of his regime with those of the former supervisor. In such a vulnerable position, this supervisor should welcome any assistance to improve his managerial appearance. The use of organization value analysis also allows the reassigned supervisor to explore fully each niche of his new organization and implement study proposals for organizational improvement. In these circumstances an organization value analysis study cannot fail to yield tangible results and must bolster the reassigned supervisor's managerial image.

Combined organization. Another lucrative area for analysis is a recently combined organization with one supervisor responsible for the merged organization. To the supervisor of such an organization, the potential benefits afforded by organization value analysis represent an opportunity not only to efficiently integrate and streamline the merged organization but also to show higher managers that their trust in him was well placed. If the results of the analysis are dramatic and he can increase the total value of the organization appreciably, he is in a favorable position to grandstand. He can impress his fellow supervisors as well as his management with his willingness to throw open his organization to a new approach, and the resultant improvements will attest to management capability superior to that of the previous supervisor. If the results of the analysis are not dramatic, the entire study bears evidence that his original planning and organization decisions leave little room for improvement.

Backlog of work. An organization that very often will welcome organization value analysis is one that has a backlog of work inconsistent with the staffing allowed or has recently been assigned additional tasks without a commensurate increase in manpower budget. In these instances the cognizant supervisor must take some action to solve his problem and is well disposed and well motivated to participate eagerly in any analysis that offers potential solutions. If the study is successful in resolving his difficulties, he becomes a better manager; if the study falls short of total improvement, the results become the basis for a logical increase in manpower. He can't lose.

An additional advantage in selecting an organization under these conditions is that the employees of the organization will be better motivated to cooperate since their jobs are in no way endangered by the study. Still another organizational condition that presents an excellent opportunity for a successful study is one whose backlog of work has increased because of a previous mandatory reduction in manpower without a reduction of tasks.

Reduction of manpower. An organization that has exceeded its assigned budget and must reduce personnel in order to achieve an on-budget condition or an organization that must reduce staff because of an arbitrary reduction in percentage of personnel does not present the most ideal circumstances for employee support in conducting a study. To expect objectivity and cooperation from employees in a study that will result in terminating some of them is absurd, and any data collected from these employees would be biased if not downright false.

The data normally collected in an organization value analysis study under ideal conditions are not always complete and not always factual because of human error and some unintentional subjectivity, but the use of data that have been intentionally falsified will not only render the analysis worthless but may also adversely influence the supervisor's subsequent decisions. In spite of these drawbacks, organization value analysis still can be of significant use to the supervisor. The mode of analysis will remain the same but the data needed to prepare OVAC are estimated by the supervisor with the assistance of his lead men. After the analysis, the supervisor will be able to select those activities that are of marginal value and reduce the staff accordingly. The functional analysis will clearly indicate the priority of each activity and task in terms of function satisfaction.

Size of organization. Another consideration in selecting an organization for study is size. Although the use of organization value analysis is not restricted by this factor, the neophyte may do well to start small. The urge to expose the overstaffed organization that has always been considered a thorn in the side should be restrained until experience has been attained in the use of OVAC.

The ideal organization to select for the learning phase is one consisting of approximately ten employees and one supervisor engaged in a fairly routine repetitive activity. This organization is large enough to permit total application of the techniques, yet it is small enough that control can be maintained. The tasks and activities of such an organization should be relatively easy to define in functional definition form compared to a very large, very complex group, and initial errors can be rectified on this level without destroying the entire study. As experience in VAMP is gained and as confidence in the analysis increases, the use of OVAC can progress to the next higher level of organization. When sufficient success has been experienced, the progression from the lowest level to the next higher level should be reversed. The potential of organization value analysis increases as the level of organization application increases.

Types of organization. The type of organization is an important factor in selecting an organization for study. One whose output is extremely diversified and whose activities are sporadic rather than constant offers considerable difficulty for the inexperienced analyst or team. The data collection phase must be stringently controlled because of the wide latitude of activity and task definition possibilities. Because of the sporadic nature of the activities and tasks, the survey period must be expanded to include one full cycle of organization activity. This may entail the development of intricate sampling plans covering a period of several months.

An organization with a varied and infrequent output is often a prime target for organization value analysis because of the lack of standards usually associated with such an organization. Until experience is gleaned, the selection of an organization for study should be confined to those that have a fairly repetitive and well-defined output.

TEAM APPROACH

The word "objectivity" has appeared in previous paragraphs frequently enough to give the impression that it is one of our most readily available commodities. Objectivity is advocated in the collection of data and in the analysis phase and is usually recommended in every business endeavor. It is the state of mind which allows a coldly logical, unemotional, unbiased evaluation of a situation—but to expect or demand its full use is extremely optimistic. To advise the analyst to use objectivity in his analysis for maximum benefits is parallel to advising the stockbroker to "make a million" in the stockmarket. In both cases he *knows* what to do and in neither case does anyone tell him *how* to do it.

Human relations experts estimate that the average individual acts in a truly logical manner approximately 10 percent of the time, which leaves 90 percent subject to human frailties. Of course, the 10 percent would vary substantially and probably in proportion to the degree of involvement and potential personal gain or loss. Since the supervisor of an organization that is to be subjected to organization value analysis is deeply involved with the study, his objectivity is in all likelihood less than desired, even when he is sufficiently motivated to participate in the study.

In order to increase the objectivity of the analysis (not necessarily the objectivity of the supervisor), other factors can be introduced by establishing a team with the concerned supervisor appointed as the team leader. The team members, two to four depending on the complexity of the organization or the availability of people, should be other supervisors who have some knowledge of the organization under study. These team members should be assigned by their managers to participate. They will add desired objectivity and also contribute to the development of activity alternates because of their widespread experience. In most cases, the team will add a desired formality to the study and preclude a superficial treatment. If the team approach is impractical or inadvisable because of circumstances, the individual performing the OVAC analysis must be mature enough to realize that the amount of prejudice he allows to slip into the analysis will be directly and adversely reflected in the study results.

Unsuitable Study Subjects

There are conditions that render some organizations not particularly susceptible to organization value analysis. They should not be subjected to OVAC until the use of VAMP techniques has gained a firm foothold in the company management policy. The organization that is to be totally reorganized in the near future should be avoided until the reorganization has been completed. Although this suggestion seems obvious, the analyst should make certain that higher management does not have any unpromulgated plans of this nature. It can be disheartening to perform a detailed study and present dramatic results to upper management, only to find that the entire concept of the organization is scheduled for change in two weeks.

An organization whose output consists of such unmeasurable abstractions as public relations, industrial relations, office programs, and advertising should also be bypassed in favor of an organization with a measurable output until substantial experience and support has been gained.

A supervisor with an indifferent attitude can present serious roadblocks to an organization value analysis of his organization. An outspoken critic can be converted to an outspoken advocate by participation in a study; a supporter can be strengthened, but an apathetic supervisor will dismiss proposed changes with a degree of rationalization rivaling that of a political candidate after elections. Although a tempting subject for VAMP, he should be avoided until a record of success has been achieved.

TRAINING

Few things are more distasteful than observing an unskilled or inept craftsman at work. Application of VAMP by the untrained can excite similar displeasure. The theory and application of techniques can be deceptively simple, but, unless individuals are exposed to some type of formal training in actual application of the techniques, their first attempt may well be their last. The normal management resistance to new but unheralded techniques is not conducive to forgiveness or second chances. The first operational VAMP study must be performed, or at least conducted, by VAMP trained personnel. Chapter 10 explains and evaluates the methods of training available personnel.

* * *

The foregoing guidelines to selecting a project for organization value analysis may appear paradoxical in view of the claims in the previous chapters concerning universal application. These guidelines, however, portray the ideal or optimum conditions of application. They are intended as a guide for introducing the concepts into a company strategically in order to create an excellent first impression and to obtain lasting management support. As management acceptance increases, the importance of guidelines for selecting a project will diminish proportionally until the concepts and practices become an inherent part of the management functions. Until this happy occasion becomes a reality, the proper selection of projects is of paramount importance.

5

OVAC Preparation

An organization value analysis study revolves around the organization value analysis chart (OVAC). This chart identifies each individual in the organization, notes the tasks he performs, and contains a list of the organization output. These data are portrayed in a revealing arrangement that facilitates analysis. The information required to prepare the chart is developed by the employees of the organization and compiled by the organization's supervisor or the study team. The collected data must reflect actual conditions, and attempts to subvert or misrepresent these conditions can deny the full potential of the study. The validity of the collected data is dependent upon the degree of planning effort.

A prerequisite to the preparation of a valid chart is motivation. The organization supervisor must be motivated to participate and his employees must be motivated to develop the needed data in a conscientious manner. The supervisor can be motivated in any number of ways, some of which are described in Chapter 4. Motivating the employees requires much thought and planning. The supervisor must assure his employees that their security will in no way be jeopardized; rather, the study results may improve job conditions and increase job interest. The importance of the information they develop must be emphasized. Withholding the truth or lying outright is never acceptable, for beyond the ethical consideration is the mundane fact that future efforts to apply value analysis of management practices will be resisted to such an extent that failure will be assured. Employees should therefore be advised of the reasons for the study and the methods to be used.

An excellent way to introduce the study is to have a senior company official serve as an icebreaker to explain the study and spell out the parameters. His presence will lend authority and formality to the survey and will motivate the employees to participate in it because they know it has company endorsement. Company authorship and sponsorship is extremely important in motivating the average employee.

Although VAMP was designed to reduce paperwork, additional forms had to be designed to collect the data for the preparation of OVAC. Three standard forms are used for this purpose—the activity list, the task data sheet, and the task list.

ACTIVITY LIST

The activity list is prepared by the organization supervisor as the first step in the study. The activities performed by the total organization are listed in order of importance. These activities consist of outputs or services performed for some other group or agent.

A good deal of reflection on the part of the supervisor is required to distinguish between an activity and a task. (This distinction is explained in subsequent paragraphs.) The listing of activities also requires a certain amount of judgment concerning the level of detail. Some activities can be dissected to such an extent that the listing becomes too cumbersome for analysis, or two or more activities can be combined, which is equally undesirable. Somewhere in between is the optimum. For example, in describing the activity of an engineering liaison organization the words "coordinate engineering data" are probably much too abstract to be useful, while "correct mechanical engineering errors on circuit board No. 12345" may be too detailed.

Unfortunately, there are no specific, quantitative criteria that can be applied universally to organizations. The supervisor must use judgment, with full realization that correctly identifying his organization's activities is the most important aspect of the study. Errors introduced at this phase multiply geometrically as the study progresses.

It has been found through experience that, for the purposes of an organization value analysis study, the number of activities for any one organization should not be more than ten or fewer than six. This is not to imply that an organization should not *have* more than ten activities, only that no more than ten should be listed. Those activities remaining after the ten most important have been selected will probably be relatively insignificant as far as cost is concerned, and they can be combined in that invaluable category, "miscellaneous."

The mere preparation of the activity list will give the supervisor more insight into his own organization. However, the activities that he selects and the importance he assigns to each are based on his *opinion* of what his organization should be accomplishing and do not necessarily represent conditions as they actually exist.

After the inputs have been received from the employees, the supervisor will usually have to remove some activities from his list. He will find that activities he believed were necessary and thought were being carried out according to his directions may not even be referred to by the employees. On the other hand, he may have to add activities to the list to encompass tasks that he was not aware were being performed. In most instances, the supervisor will have to revise his priorities to agree in part with what his employees feel are the most important activities.

Exhibit 11 is an activity list for a typical supermarket. In this example, the store manager has listed ten activities in descending order of importance to him. In terms of organization man-hours, he expects that the greatest effort will be spent in support of activity No. 1—servicing customers. The example also serves to illustrate the extensive scope of VAMP application.

Task Data Sheet

Exhibit 12 is an example of a task data sheet—the basic form used to collect and record information on the type and amount of work

Exhibit 11

OVAC ACTIVITY LIST

DEPARTMENT	SECTION	DEPT. NO.	SUPERVISOR	DATE
Supermarket	All	–	A. Peters	3/15/8

ACTIVITY NO.	ACTIVITY (VERB-NOUN)
1	Service Customers
2	Maintain Inventory Control
3	Maintain Equipment
4	Maintain Facility
5	Prepare Reports
6	Order Stock
7	Maintain Stock
8	Train Employees
9	Deliver Food
10	Miscellaneous

being done by each employee. It constitutes a complete accounting of the methods used to accomplish each activity of the organization, and it provides most of the data needed to prepare OVAC.

Each employee including the supervisor prepares one task data sheet each day for the period of the survey, the duration of which will depend on the nature of the organization. If the tasks are fairly repetitive and the work cycle is weekly, a survey lasting one week may be sufficient. If the cycle of work is monthly the survey should include one full cycle, but it may not be necessary to prepare the task data list each day of the month. In some cases sampling can be used. The organization supervisor must assure himself that the data he is collecting are truly representative of normal operating conditions, taking into consideration employee absences, vacations, and any other conditions which would bias the study.

After selecting a survey period that he believes will provide valid data, the supervisor should spend considerable time instructing the employees in preparing their task data sheets. Although not as com-

Exhibit 12

OVAC TASK DATA SHEET

DEPT.NO. Supermarket	ORGANIZATION VALUE ANALYSIS CHART TASK DATA SHEET FOR TASK LIST	NAME Tom Jones
DATE		JOB TITLE Butcher

TO GATHER DATA FOR PREPARATION OF YOUR TASK LIST, YOU MAY WISH TO KEEP TRACK OF THINGS YOU DO, IN THE COLUMNS BELOW. WRITE THE DESCRIPTION OF YOUR FIRST TASK IN THE MORNING UNDER TASK #1. THEN MARK #1 OPPOSITE ALL TIMES YOU WORK ON TASK #1. DO THE SAME FOR #2, #3, ETC. AS YOU GO THROUGH THE DAY. INTERRUPTIONS MARK A, B, ETC. IN THAT COLUMN, AND DESCRIBE UNDER "DESCRIPTION." PHONE INTERRUPTIONS, SHOW TALLY MARKS FOR EACH ONE, OPPOSITE THE TIME THEY OCCUR. IN THIS WAY YOU CAN SUMMARIZE THE DATA AT THE END OF EACH DAY, AND USE AS A GUIDE FOR YOUR TASK LIST.

TASK NO.	DESCRIPTION	TOTAL TIME	TASK NO.	DESCRIPTION	TOTAL TIME
1	Stock cases	105	11		
2	Sharpen equipment	15	12		
3	Cut meat	90	13		
4	Package meat	180	14		
5	Order meat	30	15		
6	Clean up	30		TOTAL TASK TIMES (1 TO 15) (EXCLUDING LUNCH, ETC.)	450 MIN.
7			A	INTERRUPTIONS (DETAIL IN PHONE & OTHERS HERE)	QUANTITY
8			B		
9			C		
10			D		

TIME	TASK NO.	INTERRUPTIONS A	B	C	D	MISC.	TIME	TASK NO.	INTERRUPTIONS A	B	C	D	MISC.	TIME	TASK NO.	INTERRUPTIONS A	B	C	D	MISC.
8:00	1						11:00	4						2:00	1					
:15	1						:15	4						:15	1					
:30	1						:30	4						:30	1					
:45	1						:45	4						:45	Break					
9:00	2						12:00	Lunch						3:00	4					
:15	3						:15	''						:15	4					
:30	3						:30	''						:30	4					
:45	3						:45	''						:45	4					
10:00	3						1:00	4						4:00	4					
:15	3						:15	4						:15	4					
:30	3						:30	5						:30	6					
:45	Break						:45	5						:45	6					

plex as a tax return, the sheet is open to interpretation, and each employee will interpret it differently. The law of chance that two of ten employees will see the form in an identical light does not apply, and the results, instead of yielding an orderly correlation of data, will seem to indicate that each of the ten employees works for a different company. Thus the supervisor's time spent in instructing his organization will save at least a multiple of that time in assimilating the inputs received.

The difference between an activity and a task should be understood by the employees before the task data sheets are prepared. The

Exhibit 13

ACTIVITY-TASK COMPARISON

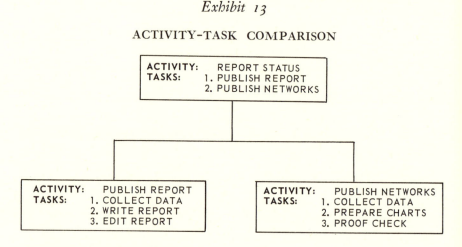

tasks are the jobs that are being done to arrive at the *activity* or organization output. It isn't easy to explain this difference because of the lack of definable boundaries. For example, the publication of a report is one *activity* of an organization, whereas the *tasks* that make up this activity are described by such terms as collecting data, writing report, editing report, printing report, and so forth. If the study were applied to the next higher level of organization, as shown in Exhibit 13, the activity in the first instance would become the task in the second instance.

The supervisor may reveal to the employees the activities he has selected. This will simplify the compilation of task data sheet information; but it will also influence the employees to fit the tasks to the activities, and a certain degree of objectivity will be sacrificed.

Another element that requires a firm and clear understanding is the degree of task detail desired. If an employee defines his tasks on the therblig level (grasp, lift, release), the supply of task data sheets will be exhausted long before the tasks are listed. For example, in one VAMP workshop seminar the instructor failed to elaborate on the importance of establishing task magnitudes. As a result, one engineering group supervisor listed 195 tasks. These did not constitute all tasks performed by his entire organization; they were just the ones he himself performed during an average week. If the study had continued at this level, it would never have been completed.

Equally objectionable is overgeneralization. If an employee says he has only one task—defined as "coordinate systems development" —and performs it eight hours per day, five days per week, he has contributed little for subsequent analysis. In some cases, this may be premeditated.

One task data sheet is prepared by each employee each day. The employee records the first task he performs in the day as Task No. 1 and records its duration in the time schedule on the lower portion of the form. If the first task consumes an hour of his time, he enters the figure "1" in the *task number* column next to the four time periods between eight and nine o'clock. When the first task has been completed and a new one begins, the employee enters this one as Task No. 2 and records the duration of this second task in the same way on the lower part of the form. Each successive task is described and the time recorded until the workday is completed. If the employee repeats a task, he does not describe it a second time; he uses the previous task-identification number to record the time in the time schedule.

Exhibit 12 is the completed task data sheet of Tom Jones, the butcher in the supermarket. His first task in the morning was to stock the cases with meat and he worked on it for one hour. He entered the description of the task—stock cases—on the first line as Task No. 1 and recorded the time spent on this task by inserting the figure "1" next to the first four time periods. The second task of the day was to sharpen the equipment, which he completed in 15 minutes. He entered the description of the task as Task No. 2 and inserted the numeral "2" in the time schedule next to the 9:00 A.M. time period. The third, fourth, and fifth tasks were recorded in order, but at 2:00 P.M. he had to restock the meat cases, which required 45 minutes. Instead of redescribing the task as No. 6, he merely entered "1" in the three time periods 2:00, 2:15, and 2:30 P.M. The same condition was repeated at 3:00 P.M., when he spent 75 minutes on Task No. 4, packaging meat.

At the end of each day the employee determines the total time spent on each task and records the time in the total-time column. The time can be recorded in minutes, tenths of hours, or fractions of hours, and all three may be used by the employees unless the supervisor establishes a standard beforehand.

When the supervisor is convinced that his employees fully understand the procedure and will return the task data sheets to him correctly and uniformly prepared, he should conduct a one-day trial. After collecting the trial task data sheets from the employees, he may feel the need to speak with each employee individually in order to explain the process in more depth. During these interviews the supervisor should review each item on the task data sheet with the employee, and they should agree upon the scope of the tasks and terminology to be used to express each task. Extreme care must be taken in these meetings to see that the employee's original descriptions of his tasks are not revised in substance to agree with what the supervisor thinks they should be. The purpose is to obtain some degree of consistency in the description and scope of a task being performed by two or more employees. When each task data sheet has been reviewed, the study can be initiated. Each employee retains his task data sheets until the end of the specified survey period, at which time he submits them to his supervisor.

Task List

The task list is the form used to record the combined total tasks performed by each employee during the survey period and to relate each task to a specific organization activity. The task lists are prepared by the supervisor from the task data sheets—one list for each employee. Exhibit 14 is the task list for Tom Jones, compiled from his task data sheets (Exhibit 12).

The first entry on the task data sheet for the first day of the survey becomes Task No. 1 on the task list. The number of times the task is performed and the total survey time devoted to it are determined by reviewing each task data sheet and adding up the number of

Exhibit 14

OVAC TASK LIST

NAME Tom Jones	JOB TITLE Butcher			DATE		
DEPARTMENT Supermarket	SECTION	DEPT. NO.		SUPERVISOR A. Peters		
TASK NUMBER	DESCRIPTION			QUANTITY	POSTED TO ACTIVITY NO.	HOURS PER WEEK
1	Stock cases			10	7	8.75
2	Sharpen equipment			5	3	1.25
3	Cut meat			1	7	7.5
4	Package meat			10	1	15.0
5	Order meat			5	6	2.5
6	Clean up			5	4	2.5
					TOTAL	37.5

times that specific task is recorded and its duration in each instance. The frequency of the task is adjusted to represent one week and is entered in the quantity column. Total time expended on the task is also factored to represent one week and is entered in the hours-per-week column. The task is then related to the organization activity it supports, and that number, taken from the activity list, is recorded in the posted-to-activity-number column. If the task cannot be related to one of the entries already on the activity list, another activity may have to be incorporated. Whether this is necessary depends upon the total time consumed by the task. If the time is relatively insignificant in proportion to the total number of hours (that is, if it is less than 1 or 2 percent), the task can be classified as miscellaneous. However, if the time consumed is greater than this, a new activity should be recorded and the activity list should be revised accordingly.

Assuming that Exhibit 11 is a recording of a typical day, the number of times the butcher performed Task No. 1 in a single week would be ten, and the total time spent on this task during a typical week would be 8.75 hours—1.75 hours per day. The figures 10 and

8.75 are entered on the task list and the previously established activities are reviewed to determine the activity related to this task. (See Exhibit 10.) "Maintain stock," which is listed as No. 7 on the activity list, appears to be the activity that this task supports, and "7" is entered in the appropriate column. Each new task is recorded on the task list in the sequence in which it appears on the task data sheets, until all tasks together with their frequency of occurrence and total expended time have been accounted for.

When the task lists have been completed, the activity list previously prepared should require some minor adjustments as a result of the unanticipated listing of some tasks. Often a new activity list is needed to reflect what *is* being done, in contrast to the original activity list which defined activities that the supervisor *thought* were being done. The completed task lists and the activity list become the data inputs to the organization value analysis chart.

ORGANIZATION VALUE ANALYSIS CHART

The preparation of the organization value analysis chart marks the completion of the investigation phase of the organization value analysis study and constitutes the starting block for the subsequent analysis. Exhibit 15, OVAC, is comparatively easy to prepare if the supporting forms—the activity list, the task data sheets, and the task lists—are completed accurately.

The title of the organization being studied is entered in the upper right-hand corner of the chart in the designated area, and a check is placed in the appropriate block indicating a display of the present organization. The supervisor is reminded by this check that the purpose of the chart is to record the actual situation, and the tendency to improve the existing organization during this phase should be strongly discouraged.

Each employee's name and job title are entered in the area provided, with the supervisor's name listed in the first column. Employees who share the same job classifications should be listed in adjacent columns to facilitate subsequent comparisons. The first entry in the body of the form is Activity No. 1. The task list of each employee is reviewed in sequence. The supervisor's task list is reviewed first. Under his name, any task that appears on the list as posted to Activity No. 1

Exhibit 15

OVAC OF SUPERMARKET: PRESENT ORGANIZATION

FUNCTIONS
BASIC (VERB-NOUN): _____
SECONDARY (VERB-NOUN): _____

ORGANIZATIONAL UNIT CHARTED: SUPERMARKET
PRESENT ORGANIZATION: ✓
PROPOSED ORGANIZATION: ____
DATE: _____

CHARTED BY: _____   APPROVED BY: _____

No.	Activity (Verb-Noun)	Hrs. per Week	Cost per Week	% of Total	A. Peters — Manager — Tasks (Individual)	Hrs. per Week	Lucy Martin — Cashier — Tasks (Individual)	Hrs. per Week	Tom Jones — Butcher — Tasks (Individual)	Hrs. per Week	Peter Tompkins — Box Boy — Tasks (Individual)	Hrs. per Week	Steve Goldman — Stock Man — Tasks (Individual)	Hrs. per Week
1	Service customers	72.5		38	Resolve complaints	7.5	Check out purchases	27.5	Package meat	15.0	Package purchases	22.5		
2	Maintain stock	46.25		25					Stock case	8.75	Wrap vegetables	3.75	Stock shelves	16.25
									Cut meat	7.5	Stock shelves	5.0	Unpack cases	5.0
3	Maintain equipment and facility	8.75		5					Sharpen equipment	1.25	Clean up	5.0		
									Clean up	2.5				
4	Prepare reports	11.25		6	Daily store report	5.0	Cash report	1.25					Inventory report	5.0
5	Purchase wholesale	10.0		5	Order stock	7.5			Order meat	2.5				
6	Miscellaneous	41.25		22	Inspect displays	1.25	Review prices	2.5			Meetings	1.25	Stamp prices	7.5
					Supervise and administer	15.0	Set up for day	2.5					Set up displays	3.75
					Check prices	3.75	Reconcile cash	2.5						
							Meetings	1.25						
	TOTAL	190.0		100		40.0		37.5		37.5		37.5		37.5

is recorded in the tasks column together with the hours per week that he expends on that task. When the supervisor's list has been checked for all the tasks associated with Activity No. 1, the task list of the employee in the adjacent column is reviewed in the same manner. After all the task lists have been reviewed and those tasks associated with Activity No. 1 have been transferred to the chart, a line is drawn across the chart to segregate that activity. Activity No. 2 is then entered and the same review is performed on every task list until all tasks associated with this activity are recorded in the appropriate columns. The process is continued until all activities and tasks have been entered. Upon completion, the activity list and the task lists should not contain any data that do not appear on OVAC.

The hours per week of each task within a particular activity are totaled and recorded in the column next to the activity description. The total hours devoted to each activity are translated into dollars and entered in the column next to the total hours. After all dollar and hour entries have been determined and totaled at the bottom of the chart, the cost per week of each activity is expressed as a percentage of the total organizational cost. If cost data are not readily available, or if the range of the study renders the addition of cost data impractical, this information can be omitted. In these instances, the percent of total is based on the hours expended.

In the example shown in Exhibit 15, the manager selects the servicing of customers as the organization's most important activity and enters it as the first activity on the chart. From his own task list he selects only one continuing task that supports this activity—specifically, resolve complaints. He calculates the time expended in this effort as 7.5 hours per week and makes the appropriate entry in his task column. He then reviews the cashier's task list and finds that one of the total tasks she performs supports Activity No. 1. This task, check out purchases, totals 27.5 hours per week; the description and the total time are entered in the cashier's task column. This process is repeated until the time of all employees has been accounted for.

The organization value analysis chart is now complete, but the visualization afforded by this display is limited. To set the stage for subsequent analysis by team effort, a more meaningful display is required. Although the supervisor has found that the data collected thus far are beneficial, interesting, and in some cases surprising, the most important quality of OVAC—visualization—has not yet been achieved. To overcome this deficiency, the data are transferred to a

Exhibit 16

DATA COLLECTION STEPS

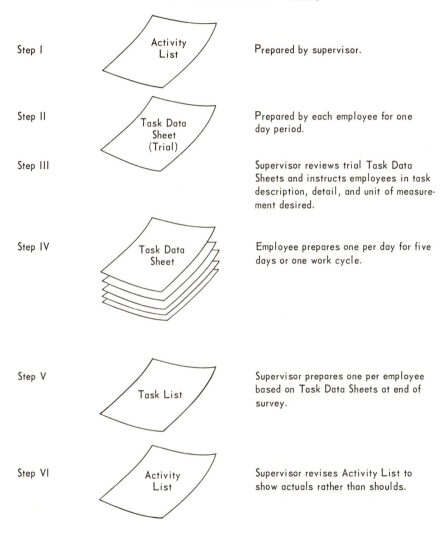

Step I — Activity List — Prepared by supervisor.

Step II — Task Data Sheet (Trial) — Prepared by each employee for one day period.

Step III — Supervisor reviews trial Task Data Sheets and instructs employees in task description, detail, and unit of measurement desired.

Step IV — Task Data Sheet — Employee prepares one per day for five days or one work cycle.

Step V — Task List — Supervisor prepares one per employee based on Task Data Sheets at end of survey.

Step VI — Activity List — Supervisor revises Activity List to show actuals rather than shoulds.

wall chart so that all team members can view the same data at the same time during the analysis discussions.

* * *

Although the data collection process may seem excessively involved, the time expended—and it does take time—is more than compensated for by the study benefits. Indeed, if the effort were to cease upon preparation of the organization value analysis chart, the benefits to the supervisor and the benefits to the employees would have justified the expense. Exhibit 16 summarizes the data collection steps required to prepare the chart.

6

OVAC Analysis

THE completed OVAC may appear to the industrial engineer as nothing more than the old work distribution chart with minor revisions and a fancy new name—an old technique, repackaged to be sold as something new. If the procedure were to end with the preparation of the organization value analysis chart, the industrial engineer's contention would be difficult to refute. The techniques used thus far to collect and present the data are those of work simplification. But the OVAC analysis takes on a completely new light with the introduction of value engineering techniques. The preparation is basically a mechanical process; the analytical phase provides the means to increase the value of what now exists.

FUNCTIONAL DEFINITIONS

The analysis begins by establishing functional definitions for the basic and secondary functions of the organization being studied. The basic function—that is, the purpose for which the organization was established—must be defined by using only two words, a noun and a verb. To explain the purpose of an organization with many words, paragraphs, or pages is relatively simple; but such explanations usually define the *activities* and *tasks* of an organization and seldom provide words specific enough for analysis. To write a two-word definition is difficult and requires considerable thought. In addition, the selection of the proper definition at the proper level of abstraction is critical because all subsequent analysis is built on or compared to the organization's basic function.

During a hardware project the value engineering team can examine the piece of hardware, understand how it supports the next higher assembly by reviewing the drawings, and disassemble the study object into its component parts. For example, if the hardware item to be studied is a motor shaft, the team might examine the shaft itself. The basic function of this item may first be defined as "transmits energy," and the value engineering team might scoff at the seminar instructor's lengthy presentation of the functional definition. How can so much time and importance be allotted to defining the function when the function is obvious? But this cursory examination of the function will lead to confusion, frustration, and cynicism about value engineering. The team that identified the basic function so quickly will have additional time to devote to the creative phase. The team members will develop alternative methods of transmitting energy and the listing may be impressive, but these alternatives will have little application to the motor shaft.

It is true that the shaft transmits energy, but the definition is too general for a value engineering study. The level of abstraction of the functional definition will provide alternate methods to accomplish that function on an equally high level of abstraction. If the basic function commensurate with the study objectives is to provide torque, the alternative methods of transmitting energy will be of little practical value and the time expended in developing them will have been wasted. More often than not, the obvious basic function defined is not the one desired. Many studies have failed simply because the team members did not give the functional definition the emphasis and consideration it requires.

Defining the basic function of an organization is a much more formidable task than defining the basic function of a piece of hardware. The organization can't be picked up, turned over, examined, or disassembled into its component parts. It is, in effect, a slippery abstraction with only those parameters that are established by OVAC. Not only the basic function but the secondary functions of the organization (other attributes that are dependent upon the basic function and that add required features) must also be given functional definition.

After the basic and secondary functions have been defined, analyzed, and evaluated, and assuming that no major revision results from the evaluation, all the activities of the organization or the most costly ones, depending upon the desired depth of the study, are subjected to the functional approach. Again, assuming that no major changes to the existing activities are dictated, the functional approach is applied to the high-cost tasks.

The definition of the basic function begins with two questions: What does it do? What is the purpose for the organization's existence? In the example of the supermarket the answer seems to be obvious, and the basic function will be recorded as "sell food." This may well describe the function of the organization in workable, specific terms. However, before developing alternate methods for the basic function, the level of abstraction of the selected definition must be analyzed further.

The process known as "the ladder of abstraction" is used to assist in determining the different levels of abstraction of the selected functional definition. To increase the level of abstraction, the question *why* the supermarket sells food is asked. The answer might be, to obtain money. This in turn prompts the query as to why it wants to obtain money, which could be answered, to provide profits. Each time the question is asked, the answer moves into an area of greater generality.

Defining the basic function in more specific terms, on the other hand, requires subjecting it to the question, "How?" Asking *how* the supermarket sells food might produce the answer—"by providing food." Asking how it provides food can be answered with the phrase, "by displaying food." Each successive answer to the question provides a functional definition that is more specific than the preceding one. The ladder of abstraction for the food-selling function, from the general to the specific, is as follows:

- Satisfy stockholders.
- Increase profit.
- Obtain money.

- Sell food.
- Provide food.
- Display food.
- Stock shelves.

The importance of choosing a function at the proper level of abstraction can be clearly demonstrated by selecting two or more of these functions and recording various other methods that could be used to satisfy each. For example, if the function is to obtain money, alternates may include: (1) borrow money; (2) invest money; (3) sell real estate; (4) sell equipment. If the function is to provide food, other methods may be listed: (1) catalog display; (2) TV scanner; (3) telephone selection; (4) purchasing plans; (5) mobile displays. The comparison of each set of alternatives will show a definite incompatibility. The methods developed to provide food, for instance, will differ radically in nature from those developed to obtain money, and the selection of ways to obtain money when the function should be to provide food will result in an unfruitful study and expensive confusion. In addition, the team members who have experienced this difficulty will not be the most ardent supporters of VAMP in the future.

After reviewing the functions appearing on the ladder of abstraction, the analyzer would probably discard the food-selling function because the organization really doesn't sell; it provides a display of foods that allows the customer to select the ones he wants. The words that best describe this condition are "provide food."

Another example illustrating the importance of selecting the proper function at the proper level of abstraction occurred during the analysis of an employee suggestion group. In the first attempt to identify the basic function of the group, the study team unanimously agreed that it was to improve morale. Since this basic function was so conspicuous, the team members decided to develop abstractions to this choice as further proof of their adroitness. The whys and hows were dutifully employed and the ladder was constructed as follows:

- Increase profits.
- Save money.
- Increase efficiency.
- Improve morale.

- Reward employees.
- Evaluate suggestions.

Each of the listed functions was examined fully, and the examination made it clear that to increase morale might well be the basic function of the employee suggestion *program*, but it certainly was not the basic function of the employee suggestion *group*. The basic function to evaluate suggestions was the only one that specifically identified the purpose of the group's existence. This exercise had an important corollary benefit. It highlighted the potential danger of transferring the object of investigation—the organization being studied—to a higher level of abstraction. The parent organization of the group being studied or the program being conducted by the group may have exciting cost-reduction potentials, but the temptation to go off on this tangent should be deferred until the existing study has been completed.

Once defined, the basic function is exposed to creative thinking, since its cost has already been estimated on OVAC. What other ways can this function be satisfied? Each team member is urged to reveal any ideas he thinks could in any way contribute to the fulfillment of the basic function, regardless of their practicality. These ideas are recorded on some visual aid such as a chalkboard or a flip chart that is visible to the entire team. All judgment concerning the suggestions is suspended until each member of the team has exhausted his supply of ideas.

In the cited example of the supermarket, alternative ways of fulfilling the basic function—provide food—might include an automated system where the customer could remain in her car and select food by dropping prepunched cards in a central hopper. A TV scanner would provide price and availability and an automated inventory system could select, package, and deliver the items to her car. Another idea would be home delivery in response to telephone requests.

As ideas are recorded they often prompt new ideas or variations on ideas already noted. When the creative phase has been exploited to the extent practical, each listed idea is evaluated and either rejected or deferred for further investigation.

An investigation of the automated supermarket idea would reveal that present labor costs could be reduced. The need for cashiers would disappear because credit cards would be attached to pre-punched data processing cards. The jobs performed by the box boys and stock men in stocking the shelves could be eliminated. The building, furniture, and fixtures could be much less lavish. But would the typical customer ever be able to accept the cantaloupe without first smelling it or buy the tomato without seeing or feeling it? This idea might be deferred for a psychological and cost-feasibility study. Others may be rejected quickly, or the entire listing may be rejected and the existing method pronounced the one most economically feasible.

If a radical alternative is chosen to satisfy the basic function, further analysis of the existing organization ceases. Efforts are then turned to the new method. Activities and tasks are added in sufficient quantity and scope to make it workable. The proposed organization is spelled out on an OVAC wall chart to aid implementation. Theoretically, maximum cost benefits will be realized when a new and ingenious approach is devised to fulfill the basic function. However, the analyzer should not despair when this does not occur. In many instances the existing method will be continued, sometimes because the team members are reluctant to wipe out an entire organization. The most practical benefits of the overall analysis will become evident during the analysis of the activities.

ACTIVITY ANALYSIS

The total cost of a typical organization is not allocated equally to all activities. In fact, a major portion of the cost is usually associated with relatively few activities. These are the ones that deserve thorough analysis and evaluation. They were previously identified on the chart in order of importance to the organization manager, and it would be normal to assume that the cost of each would decrease in proportion to its stated importance. The analyzer will find that this correlation is seldom reflected in the organization value analysis chart. Often the activities listed third, fourth, and fifth in order of importance will appear as first, second, and third, in order of cost. The incongruity itself provides additional reasons for using organization value analysis.

The most expensive activity in terms of hours or cost is reduced to a functional definition. Although an effort is made to describe the activity in two words during the original listing, it does not follow that the two words selected constitute a functional definition. The activities of many organizations will be defined with management jargon at a level of abstraction that precludes serious analysis. These activities are described in language commonly used in any industrial organization: control program, analyze systems, integrate testing, verify quality, coordinate reviews, direct activities. Abstract terminology such as this must be translated into more specific terms by a functional definition.

Activity Evaluation

A functional definition is established for the most costly activity with the same care and thoroughness used to define the basic function of the organization. The function is evaluated by comparing it to the basic and secondary function of the organization. The evaluation of the function's worth in this case is judgmental, not purely mathematical. If the hours consumed by the most costly activity directly support the *basic* function of the organization, the activity is said to have good value. If the same activity supports only a *secondary* function, the cost-to-function ratio indicates poor value. If the activity does not support either the basic or secondary functions, it obviously has no value and should be eliminated. This degree of value serves as a broad standard against which different ways to accomplish the function of the activity can be measured.

Elaborate tables and charts could be developed using weight factors that would assign numerical values to the activities. Such instruments would relieve the analyzer of the judgmental appraisal of good and poor value, but it would place a tremendous burden on the person who devised such tables or charts. It is comparable to the early PERT charts and the technique of establishing time estimates of the activities on a PERT network. By subjecting to a statistical formula a series of estimates of optimistic, pessimistic, and most-likely times, a supposedly valid estimate was achieved. Eventually these cumbersome calculations gave way to the one estimate by the individual most qualified to judge the duration of an activity.

In evaluating the worth of an activity in organization value analysis, it would be difficult to show that the validity of activity standard charts was equal to or greater than the best estimate of the analyzer. A certain degree of subjective judgment must be applied at some level. It seems reasonable that validity will increase with the evaluator's level of knowledge of the item being studied. The labels applied to the worth of any activity are merely guides in the creative thinking process.

When the most costly function has been evaluated, the OVAC activity/task analysis sheet is used to foster an orderly and complete creative thinking phase. (See Exhibit 17.) The activity is identified by its number, and the cost in either hours or dollars is recorded. The description of the activity is noted by entering the functional definition previously established. The creative phase explores all possible methods to satisfy the functional definition, listing each on the analysis sheet as it is suggested by a team member.

The analysis sheet can accommodate ten alternates, which is by no means the optimum. Depending upon the team members and their backgrounds, the number of choices can climb into the hundreds. The greater the number, the more chances there are of uncovering a unique or ingenious method of accomplishing the function at a drastic decrease in cost. Again, during the development of the alternates, *all* judgment concerning their merit or practicality is suspended. When all have been listed and the creative phase has been exploited to the satisfaction of the team members, the team evaluates the suggestions. Each one is either accepted for further investigation, rejected, or accepted as it appears on the list.

Those deferred for study and those accepted are scrutinized further. The two or three that appear to have the best potential for successful implementation are listed on the lower part of the analysis sheet and their cost is estimated. The cost estimate of each alternate is compared with the cost of the present activity while considering the value rating of the activity's basic function. If the value rating is poor and the differences in cost between the selected alternates and the present methods are slight, the creative phase will have to be repeated. New alternates must be developed and examined until one is found that offers a substantial decrease in cost. If the value rating is good, a reduction in cost of 15 to 30 percent could be considered adequate. This evaluation of costs versus value rating is likely to reduce the choices to one or two.

The completed analysis sheet is set aside and the second most expensive activity is analyzed and evaluated in the same manner. This process continues until all the activities have been evaluated and an analysis sheet has been completed for each. The last entry in the activity column will usually be "miscellaneous," which covers all the

Exhibit 17

OVAC ACTIVITY/TASK ANALYSIS SHEET

ACTIVITY NO. _____ COST PER WEEK $ _____

TASK _____

_____

ALTERNATES

1	
2	
3	
4	
5	
6	
7	
8	
9	

SELECTION	EST. COST
1	
2	
3	

hours not specifically identified with an activity. This catchall, of course, cannot be evaluated as an activity, but its impact on the total cost of the organization should be examined. If the time or cost in this category exceeds 10 percent of the organization's total, each task within the category should be reviewed to insure that it does not support one of the listed activities. If a task has been listed erroneously, the chart should be revised accordingly. Also, if the miscellaneous tasks are similar, perhaps an activity has been overlooked.

The depth of the functional evaluation will be decided by the interaction of many variables. If the results of the activity analysis are sufficiently fruitful, there may be no need to explore the tasks. The activity alternates selected to replace the existing activities, if substantially different, will probably void all existing tasks and require the development of new tasks to accomplish the new activity.

Another constraint can be the time available to complete the study. Organization value analysis is not a wonder drug that will automatically cure any organizational malady. It requires time and effort, which is limited in many instances. If the functional evaluation does not produce the desired results at this point, its continuation into the task level is recommended—at least for the high-cost tasks. If the task-level analysis proves futile, the team members may congratulate each other for discovering the perfect organization.

The example of the supermarket was designed to illustrate a typical organization and did not include premeditated incongruities. It is reasonable and on the surface provides little opportunity for improvement. Yet the functional approach, if applied to the activities, will highlight areas of high cost and poor value. For example, the most expensive activity of the supermarket is the first one, "service customers." This agrees with the manager's rating as the most important activity. This activity is challenged using the following ladder of abstraction:

- Increase profit.
- Collect dollars.
- Increase patronage.
- Impress customers.
- Service customers.
- Assist customers.

This illustrates that the lowest level of abstraction, to assist customers, offers the most specific description. To become more specific than this would entail describing each task. When the function of assisting customers is evaluated and compared to the basic function of the organization, which is to provide food, the comparison results in a value rating of poor. The function does not support providing food; it supports the secondary function of maintaining image. Therefore, the most expensive activity (also appraised by the manager as the most important) does not assist in fulfilling the primary purpose of the organization. This condition warrants substantial analysis to determine alternative low-cost methods or to eliminate the activity. Alternate choices to assisting customers may include such items as reducing the cause of complaints, self-checkout with credit card, and automatic packaging. Until the cost of this activity is reduced to a point commensurate with a secondary function of the organization, the value of the function remains poor.

Activity No. 2 on OVAC, maintain stock, is the next most expensive activity; since it directly supports the basic function of the organization, a value rating of good would be assigned. Activities No. 3 and No. 4 support secondary functions, are relatively inexpensive, and are likely to be considered good value. Activity No. 5 supports the basic function and also would be rated as good value. The miscellaneous category constitutes 22 percent of the total cost and would require substantial investigation and revision because of its size.

In reviewing the total organization, the analyzer can readily see the benefits of organization value analysis. The functional approach applied to an apparently logical and effective organization reveals that only 29 percent of the total effort is expended in accomplishing the primary purpose of the organization. This condition is akin to purchasing an item for $29 and paying delivery charges of $71, which would hardly be considered cost-effective.

PROPOSED ORGANIZATION

Almost as important as analyzing and evaluating the existing organization is the development of the proposed organization. This is not an automatic fallout from the evaluation phase. Although the pieces of the puzzle may be available, patience, time, and thought are essential ingredients in this construction task. An organization value analysis chart is used to record the buildup.

The preparation of the new OVAC begins with the recording of the basic and secondary functions in the form heading together with the organization's identifications. Each activity analysis sheet is reviewed and the one best alternate is selected as the new activity. Those selected constitute the building blocks of the proposed organization. The most important activity is entered first on the chart.

The importance of each activity is established by the function it supports. The most important should be the one that supports the basic function and requires the largest expenditure; this should be followed by the next costly activity that supports the basic function. Those that support the secondary functions are then listed in descending order of cost.

After the first activity is entered, the tasks required to perform it must be evolved, identified, assigned, and estimated. What tasks are necessary to make this new idea work, and what classification of employees is needed to perform these tasks? As each is identified, it is entered in a task column and the classification of the individual needed to perform it is inserted in the job title block at the top of the column. The estimated time required per week is also recorded with each task. When all the tasks required to accomplish the first activity are recorded in the appropriate columns, each successive activity is reviewed in the same manner until all activities have been provided for. With the addition of a miscellaneous factor, OVAC becomes the basis for staffing the proposed organization. The chart is completed by compiling the cost of each activity and the percentage of total time consumed by each, as shown in Exhibit 18.

The completed new OVAC does not mark the study termination. A final review is necessary to insure an integrated organization capable of fulfilling the assigned essential function. This final review is similar to the cursory review conducted during a typical work distribution study, consisting of three separate views. In the first view, the activities are examined to make certain that each is being performed by the proper organization. Previous use of the functional approach has established the necessity of the activities, but the entire activity may be performed more efficiently by a different organization. For instance, a training activity or a personnel activity may be more eco-

Exhibit 18

OVAC OF SUPERMARKET: PROPOSED ORGANIZATION

FUNCTIONS
BASIC (VERB-NOUN): Provide Food
SECONDARY (VERB-NOUN): Provide TV Display

ORGANIZATIONAL UNIT CHARTED: SUPERMARKET
DATE:

PRESENT ORGANIZATION
PROPOSED ORGANIZATION ✓

CHARTED BY: ___ APPROVED BY: ___

ACTIVITY NUMBER	ACTIVITY (VERB-NOUN)	HRS. PER WEEK	COST PER WEEK	% OF TOTAL	A. Peters — Systems Analyst TASKS (INDIVIDUAL)	HRS. PER WEEK	P. Tompkins — Packaging Engineer TASKS (INDIVIDUAL)	HRS. PER WEEK	Tom Jones — Meat Consultant TASKS (INDIVIDUAL)	HRS. PER WEEK
1	Fill Orders	60		63	Program Equipment	10	Control Automatic Select Equipment	15	Package Meat	20
									Cut Meat	10
							Manual Fill as Required	5		
2	Maintain Equipment	22		23	Maintain Surveillance of TV Equipment	10	Repair Equipment	6	Sharpen Equipment	2
							Perform Preventive Maintenance	4		
3	Maintain Display	10		10	Update TV Display	5				
					Check Prices	5				
4	Miscellaneous	4		4	Review EDP Reports	4				
	TOTAL	96		100		34		30		32

nomically performed by service departments established for that specific purpose, or a data collection activity may be transferred to the EDP group. What is more, the possibility of procuring services from an outside vendor specializing in a particular service should not be overlooked.

The second view concerns the tasks associated with each activity. Each task associated with Activity No. 1 is questioned to be sure that the task is being performed in the best sequence, that the employee performing the task is the one most suited to perform it, that the frequency of the task is optimum, and that the task is being performed in the simplest way. When these points have been affirmed by the evaluators or the required revisions have been incorporated in

Exhibit 19

OVAC ANALYSIS PROCESSING STEPS

ORGANIZATION ANALYSIS

- Develop functional definition for basic function.
- Develop functional definition for secondary functions.
- Develop alternates to basic function.
- Evaluate alternates.
- Select best alternate.
- If selection is radical, develop activities and tasks.
- If not, analyze activities.

ACTIVITY ANALYSIS

- List activities in order of cost.
- Analyze activities, progressing from highest to lowest cost.
- Develop functional definition.
- Assign value rating.
- Develop alternates to basic function.
- Evaluate alternates.
- Select best alternate.
- If selection is radical, develop supporting task.
- If not, analyze tasks.

TASK ANALYSIS

- List tasks in order of cost.
- Analyze highest cost activity first.
- Develop function definition.
- Assign value rating.
- Develop alternates to basic function.
- Evaluate alternates.
- Select best alternate.

PROPOSED OVAC

- Develop new OVAC incorporating proposed improvements.

FINAL REVIEW

- Review activities for proper location.
- Review tasks within activities.
- Review tasks for each employee.

OVAC, the review progresses to the tasks associated with the remaining activities until all of them have been reviewed.

The final view is one that concerns each employee of the organization and the tasks he performs. Its purpose is to insure maximum utilization of skills and a continuity in the employees' total workload. In this individual evaluation, the tasks are examined to preclude potential morale problems. The monotony of a job, the job enlargement and promotion potential, the emotional suitability of the individual to the task, and the skills required and available are all considered for optimum efficiency and employee satisfaction. Upon completion of this review, the OVAC analysis is considered to be complete.

The OVAC analysis is the efficient cause of organization value improvement and should not be slighted because of inconveniences or level of difficulty. Each step in the analysis procedure, summarized in Exhibit 19, should be followed for maximum benefits, for the omission of one may destroy the validity of the entire study.

7

Benefits of Organization
Value Analysis

IF properly conducted, an organization value analysis study will result in a degree of reorganization. Reorganization, of course, is not a new concept originated by organization value analysis. In A.D. 66 Petronius Arbiter, deputy controller to Nero, wrote:

> We trained hard . . . but it seemed that every time we were beginning to form up into teams, we would be reorganized. I was to learn later in life that we tend to meet any new situation by reorganizing . . . and a wonderful method it can be for creating the illusion of progress while producing confusion, inefficiency, and demoralization.

Perhaps Nero's reign saw excessive reorganization, but an industrial status quo would be equally devastating. In a dynamic economic environment, reorganization to cope with changing circumstances is indispensable to business longevity. The merits of this dynamic condition, termed progress, can be argued in economic terms, philosophical terms, and psychological terms, but it *is* occurring and from all indications will continue to occur at an ever increasing rate. So it must be confronted.

The reason many reorganizations are viewed with the cynicism of Petronius Arbiter is the haphazard way in which they are accomplished. Often, reorganization is undertaken with no more analytical prowess than most people use to break the bank in a roulette game. In either case success depends on chance. If the hopes of the gambler and the reorganizer are not realized with the first spin of the wheel, they try again and again until success is achieved or their funds are exhausted. Organization value analysis supplies the means to provide for required changes in a logical and economically feasible manner, without resort to the methods of the gambler.

Organization value analysis was created primarily to optimize the value of an existing organization—to allow the organization to accomplish the purpose for which it was established at a lower cost or with a higher degree of efficiency. Depending upon the circumstances, other benefits may also become evident which might even exceed the primary ones in importance.

STAFFING A NEW ORGANIZATION

The staffing proposed for a new organization can be based on any of a great many interesting techniques, one of which is clairvoyance. To the question, "How many men will you need in a department to control drawing changes?" the hopeful manager of the department may reply: "Between 35 and 40." The surprising thing about this estimate is the speed with which it is produced. For some reason the retort, "I don't know, but I'll investigate" is frowned upon as indecisive, and indecision is unbecoming to a forceful manager. The manager decides 35 to 40 is a good number and all these employees will be fully utilized in performing the control task. If 80 employees or 18 were requested, they too would all be kept busy controlling drawing changes.

Another very popular technique used in staffing a new organization is the cold, dispassionate, analytical method of adding people until a desired output is reached. The logic in this method is that the amount of output can be equated with the number of employees. Thus when the task is being accomplished the manager knows he has the correct number of people.

A third and more realistic method used in staffing a new organization is the comparison method. The manager can compare the task to be accomplished with a similar task already being done by another department. The staffing of that department becomes the basis for staffing the new organization. He may also draw on the advice of others or consult organization manuals and handbooks. This method does attempt to evaluate the organization's requirements.

The first instance, the *clairvoyance method*, is devoid of reason and cannot survive in an environment of keen competition. The method of *equating output with people* has gained a strong foothold in some industries and bureaucracies, and it may therefore be difficult to dislodge. It results from a lack of analysis primarily because of the absence of analytical tools. If the job is being performed and some profit is being made, criticism is difficult unless the critic can propose a better evaluation technique. In the typical *comparison method*, the manager in most cases uses the best information available to evaluate his manpower requirements, but seldom are tangible values assigned to the elements of the proposed work output. Implicit in this method is the assumption that the organization already in operation is cost-effective and not arbitrarily staffed. This can be a dangerous assumption.

In the instances just cited, there is a distinct possibility of over-staffing. Since the manager has no established standards, he may very well add a safety factor of 10 or 15 percent to what he considers necessary staffing. Organization value analysis provides a means to diminish substantially the potential danger of overstaffing by—

1. Determining the essential function of the new organization.
2. Establishing activity functions that support the essential functions.
3. Establishing individual tasks that contribute to the activity functions. This becomes the basis for personnel staffing.
4. Providing the organizer with more planning objectivity by using a study team.

Reducing an Existing Organization

Although a reduction in personnel is not the ideal reason for using organization value analysis, the flexibility of this procedure permits its beneficial use even here. When a business decline requires a reduction in the workforce, a planning paradox can develop. To offset the decline the company must bid on more work. But to bid competitively labor costs must be reduced; and when that has been done the capability to perform the work may be seriously impaired, resulting in an unprofitable business venture. This could require further reductions in the workforce. Although this is a gross oversimplification, the problem of cutting off organizational fat without cutting the muscle does exist.

To expect the employees of an organization to assist honestly and enthusiastically in a study that quite probably will eliminate their jobs is unrealistic, and the usual method of soliciting their help to conduct the study can be abandoned. However, an organization value analysis study can be conducted by the manager, either by himself or with the assistance of other managers. The chart can be prepared by the manager using his knowledge of the organization and, even though the prepared OVAC may deviate from the actual one in a minor degree, the subsequent analysis can be very valuable. In some instances, the manager can require the employees to assist in the study by preparing daily task data sheets which, although biased, can be factored to represent actual conditions. The judgment used in factoring will determine the study validity.

Ordinarily, a reduction in the workforce is accomplished by edict. An order comes from the top: "As of April 10, all departments will reduce manpower by 10 percent." For the inefficient but farsighted manager, this edict poses no problems. He has already programmed for this event by overstaffing his organization and has carried the surplus for just such an occasion. He can respond quickly and can tell management, "I don't know how I'll keep up with the work, but for the good of the company I'll find a way." He survives the reduction as a hero in the eyes of top management. "Why don't we have more managers of that caliber?" asks the president.

Meanwhile the efficient manager is being penalized. Following good management practices, he has provided only for the task at hand and a reduction of 10 percent will severely affect his organization's ability to perform its assigned tasks. But he will learn from this experience. The next time he staffs an organization, he, too, will provide for the potential cutbacks by inflating his requirements by the normal reduction percentage (always in units of five). The net result will be an expensive, overstaffed organization. Only when a company has an entire staff of inefficient managers can an across-the-board cut be accomplished without losing value.

This wasteful practice of overstaffing can be eliminated by organization value analysis, using OVAC as a surgical tool. The evaluation of the chart will highlight the marginal or low-value activities and tasks when viewed in relation to the essential function. Using Pareto's law of maldistribution, optimum organization value can be maintained during any progressive reduction in the workforce.

MANAGEMENT BY OBJECTIVES

In recent years a new management technique has swept American industry—management by objectives. It consists of establishing measurable objectives at all levels of organization and directing all effort to the fulfillment of these objectives. The acceptance of this technique puzzles some managers, who think only objectives *can* be managed. Nevertheless, management by objectives is a necessary part of the management vocabulary. Organization value analysis, through the use of OVAC, automatically establishes organization objectives and does it in a much more specific manner. The level of abstraction selected in management by objectives may not be sufficiently specific for meaningful measurement because of the difficulty in defining an objective without a functional definition. The vernacular of management will appear somewhere in the definitions. With these abstract definitions, each manager will know *what* he is supposed to do but still may not know *when* he has accomplished the objective.

Organization value analysis provides all the benefits of management by objectives and adds a few benefits of its own. Not only does it guarantee that the organizational objectives will be stated at a specific, measurable level, but the worth of the listed objectives is also evaluated, and each is assigned a value rating. The value rating establishes a priority of importance.

PROGRAM PLAN

The most powerful management tool in existence is probably the program plan. It is also the least used because of the effort required to produce it. The program plan is a delineation of the management functions necessary to accomplish specific objectives. It contains all the elements needed to insure attainment of the desired goals at the desired time. Although organization value analysis does not accomplish the function of a program plan per se, its contribution to the development of the plan can be substantial.

For the planning phase of the program plan, OVAC will supply the organizational objectives, the activities required to accomplish the objectives, and the tasks necessary to satisfy the activities. Supplementing OVAC with a time schedule essentially completes the planning phase.

The organizing phase, which consists of gathering together the resources needed to implement the planning phase, is partially developed by OVAC in terms of manpower staffing and will also assist in identifying the non-personnel-related resources that are required. Evaluating the tasks performed by each individual listed on OVAC may uncover certain motivational needs or potential morale problems.

The management function of control is greatly assisted by OVAC. Standards of performance developed by the chart can be of significant value in establishing control points or key milestone criteria against which actual results can be measured.

The effort required to develop a program plan at any level or in any organization can be appreciably reduced by organization value analysis with a corresponding increase in the validity and quality of the plan.

HUMAN RELATIONS

The human relations aspects of an organization value analysis study are the answer to the industrial relations manager's prayer. In an attempt to develop increased rapport between the supervisor and the employee, instruction courses in supervisory techniques have been conducted, pamphlets on coaching and appraisal methods have been published, and books on communication have been written. As a last resort, the employee performance appraisal becomes company policy; quarterly, semiannually, or annually, each supervisor confronts each of his employees in a formal tête-à-tête. During this brief meeting the supervisor describes the employee's strong points in glowing terms, criticizes his weaknesses in the softest and most nebulous terms, and rates his overall performance as below average, average, or above average. A handshake terminates the meeting and the employee leaves with praise still ringing in his ears. At the same time the supervisor thinks, "I certainly got through to him this time concerning his marginal performance." The result, another period of misunderstanding and grounds for a potential morale problem.

When conducting an organization value analysis study, in contrast, the supervisor is forced to talk to each of his employees *not* in the condescending niceties of an interview but in a man-to-man discussion evaluating the *job*, not the person. Both men discuss the aspects of the tasks being performed—the problem encountered by the employee and the desires of the supervisor. During the discussion the employee learns exactly what is expected of him and how his particular job relates to the organization's objectives. It affords him an opportunity to align his objectives with those of the organization. He learns where he is going and why. The supervisor, in turn, gains a better understanding of both the job being performed by the employee and the employee himself. Since the discussion is not being recorded for personnel files and is not used as a basis for a salary increase, the dialogue is likely to be spiced with candor. From a human relations standpoint, the rapport developed by the meetings imposed by organization value analysis have far greater value to the employee, the supervisor, and the company than the traditional periodic performance appraisal.

WORK MEASUREMENT

The industrial engineering technique of work measurement compares actual work unit output to a predetermined standard of performance. It is used primarily in areas of direct labor—repetitive factory jobs that can be measured by a stopwatch and assigned absolute value. Several attempts have been made to expand its scope into the indirect areas of clerical, service, or support jobs, but the degree of success has been substantially lower than that experienced in direct areas. The basic problem was developing the standards.

In some cases the actual output from these areas could be measured, but the basic problem remained. What should the output level be? How many design concepts should be reduced to drawings? How many financial audits should be completed per week, per month, or per year? These are difficult questions to answer, if they can be answered at all. However, some standard of performance must be established to make appraisal possible. How can an employee's performance be adjudged marginal if there is nothing against which his performance can be compared? If unit output standards are impractical in certain areas, yardsticks can be established in other terms such as cost, time, and progress toward goals.

The burden of establishing a set of criteria in these areas can be eased by organization value analysis studies. For a properly prepared OVAC will establish what the individual tasks should be in terms of cost and frequency. Regardless of the nature of the organization or the type of activity being studied, OVAC contains sufficient detailed information to form the basis for a valid work measurement system. Measurement is part of living and all achievement is the result of some form of measurement. Why should it be relegated to only the factory operations in business endeavors?

Another industrial engineering technique, job loading, is adequately provided for in organization value analysis. OVAC analysis and evaluation develops proper task continuity. The analysis of each employee's tasks will result in optimum use of skills, equitable work loading, and optimum work flow. Again, the major benefits are derived from the use of OVAC in indirect areas where little success has been attained in the past using conventional methods.

TRAINING

Organization value analysis is an excellent and effective training device. As was said earlier, the employee learns more about his own job, how it relates to associated jobs, and what part he plays in achieving organizational objectives. With this peripheral knowledge, the employee is much better equipped to perform his tasks in an efficient manner and to suggest new and less costly methods of operation.

The real cost of training a new employee is incurred during the employee's orientation period, which will range from one week to several months in duration, depending upon the level of job difficulty. During this period the employee is relatively unproductive and as such does not contribute to the company's profit. This unproductive period is not caused by the employee's lack of skill in performing the task for which he was hired. Rather, it is due to the time required for him to correlate his tasks with those of others so he can use his skills effectively. To reduce the cost to the company, this period should be lessened, and in this OVAC can assist. Instead of cloistering the new employee for a few days with the organization manual and company policy and procedure manuals, OVAC can be used. Once prepared, it provides an easily digested overview of the organization in understandable terms and allows the new employee to relate his tasks to those of the organization.

Supervisory training can be greatly enhanced by using OVAC as a training instrument. An organization value analysis study almost guarantees that the supervisor of an organization being studied will gain greater insight into his own organization. Most supervisors believe they are aware of every task being performed by each of their employees. They would be poor supervisors if they did not believe this. But new tasks appear, and obsolete and unnecessary tasks continue to be performed without the supervisor's knowledge. An existing organization's OVAC will undoubtedly generate comments of surprise and disbelief from the supervisor. During the study, he will acquire a fairly fundamental knowledge of each task being performed by his organization.

The new supervisor will find OVAC invaluable in guiding him through the early period of adjustment. Rather than having to rely on the many interpretations of how the organization should proceed, he can simply refer to his organization roadmap—OVAC. The activities will tell him where he is going; the tasks will indicate how he is going; and, most important, the basic function will tell him why he is going. The only thing left for the new supervisor to do is to provide the motivation. With OVAC, it is possible to eliminate the constant sifting of information from the employees that is usually necessary in appraising actual conditions.

Organization value analysis can also be used to advantage in attaining some of the objectives of an overall management upgrading program. This program, designed to insure an adequate supply of new supervisors and continued advancement for existing supervisors, leans heavily upon informal but planned training. The prospective supervisor must be given an opportunity to develop his potential and the existing supervisor must be afforded the occasion to expand his knowledge of company operations, thereby increasing his value to the company. A team study satisfies both. While participating in the study, the supervisor is exposed to the operating modes of other organizations in depth. The additional knowledge he gains increases his management capability. The study also provides an opportunity for the supervisory candidate to manage the organization during the time the supervisor is engaged in the study.

Even if there were no cost saving or value improvements involved in organization value analysis, the training aspects alone would more than justify the development and application of the discipline.

IMPROVED MORALE

Using the word "morale" to indicate a mood of agreement, it is probably safe to say that organization value analysis contributes to its increase. The team approach demands involvement, which usually instills a certain sense of camaraderie in the team members. The members begin to understand and respect each other's opinions. Cooperation is stimulated in working toward the immediate common goals of the study, and, more important, this cooperation is continued in future relationships. The rapport established among the supervisory team members during a study can promote the efficient attainment of other company objectives.

The morale of the participating employee is also affected; and, if the study is conducted under suitable business conditions, the effect will be positive. The employee's daily tasks, which previously only he considered important, are now being considered important by the company, thus heightening his interest and improving his morale.

FLEXIBILITY

A very important feature of organization value analysis is its extreme flexibility of application. Previous discussions concerning its capability and its uses have been restricted mainly to discrete elements of organization, but ideally and logically the analysis should begin at the highest order of organization. Yet the flexibility of organization value analysis permits its introduction at any organizational level.

Exhibit 20

ORGANIZATION VALUE ANALYSIS PROGRESSION

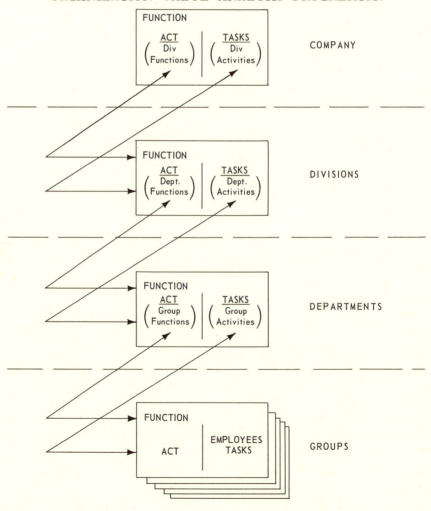

The degree of detail also can be varied in proportion to the specific purpose of the study and the amount of time available to carry it out. The president can use OVAC in a cursory analysis of the entire company, the vice president can use it for his department, and the manager can use it for his organization. The lower the level of organizational use, the more detailed the study must become to be of value. Exhibit 20 is a simplified illustration of the logical study progression.

Because of the flexibility of organization value analysis, local conditions can be accommodated. If circumstances preclude beginning the study in the board room at corporate headquarters, the analysts can start at a more practical level and use the success attained at the lower level as an incentive for expanding to the next higher and next lower levels.

* * *

The most important benefit that can evolve from the application of organization value analysis is the development of an attitude of constructive discontent in the study participants. Immediate study success is important, but the long-term gains offered by this discipline will develop a value sensitivity in management that will be transmitted to every phase of business. The extensive use of the functional approach must result in optimum return on investment.

8

Procedure Value Analysis

Nothing is more hallowed in business or more difficult to change than a procedure. Whether written or oral, the procedure enjoys a mystic quality that defies change or even questioning. Its longevity borders on that of the divine. The question, Why is it done that way? is a rhetorical one; the answer is always that the procedure says it should be. The procedure is the key to conformance. It is a guide to consistent operation and is essential to a profitable business venture.

The procedure provides for organizational conformity. Without conformity man cannot survive. Even social nonconformists dress in similar garb and in general manage to maintain an unkempt appearance in an organized and conforming manner—an organization of nonconformists. The potential danger of organizational conformance is not inherent in its existence. Rather, the danger lies in the degree and the direction the conformity may take.

Procedures are essential in attaining the desired degree of conformity, and those who advocate a freewheeling management have not reflected sufficiently on the logical effects of management without procedures.

Procedures are double-edged. They can save a great deal of money and they can cause severe financial loss. They save money by—

1. Insuring compliance with company policy.
2. Providing a guide for handling recurring actions consistently.
3. Reducing operational and functional errors.
4. Serving as a training aid for new employees.
5. Providing for a continuity of action when changes in organization and personnel occur.
6. Eliminating snap judgments in matters of policy.
7. Providing a record of standing practices for easy reference.

These are the benefits that procedures can provide if used only as needed and only to the required degree. Unfortunately, procedures can be excessively expensive as well. The following are some of the many causes of high-cost, poor-value procedures.

1. There is a penchant to overcontrol in many companies which seems to increase with the size of the company. Procedures are prepared in much detail and provide for any contingency, even though the possibility of deviation is remote and insignificant. The creation of duplicate files and complex data control systems to insure instant availability of information is common. Seldom are cost trade-offs considered. As a result a costly system often is developed to obviate the need to search for missing data, although conducting such a search when necessary would be of minor cost.

2. Paper also has a certain magnetism or allure that makes each employee a collector. Everyone wants to have a written record or a copy of each business transaction regardless of its relevance or potential use. For that reason, many distribution lists cover more area on paper than does the message itself. This tendency has an undesirable impact on company profit.

3. Often a procedure is developed to provide for temporary conditions or deviations. However, nothing is more permanent than a temporary procedure. A cursory review of a typical company proce-

dure manual will attest to this. It is as though the cancellation of an obsolete procedure were in violation of company policy and deserved disciplinary action. Aggravating this situation are apathetic employees who follow procedures blindly without questioning their purpose or practicality. For these people, procedures represent security and freedom from having to think creatively. The procedures themselves can produce this atmosphere, or the atmosphere can produce the need for the procedures. It is difficult to ascertain which is the cause and which the effect.

4. There are those individuals whose livelihood depends on procedure proliferation. The sole task of many organizations within industry and government is the generation of procedures. In fact, this generation is rapidly becoming a profession, as witness the frequent advertisements for procedure writers. While these organizations are necessary, their unbridled appetite for paper can be the cause of unnecessary procedures.

5. For those who dislike accepting the responsibility for their decisions, procedures offer myriad convenient scapegoats. They can be used to justify logical but unpleasant actions, and identifying these actions with company procedures transfers responsibility to the procedure writers.

6. The increased use of computers in industry and government gives many the opportunity to devise procedure programs containing a great deal of information, little of which is ever put to use. Computerization of a simple control system or procedure which can be processed more economically by hand increases the importance of the procedure as well as of the procedure guardian. An added feature of computerization is permanence. Once the data bits of this simple system have been electronically cast in mylar tape with a backup supply of punched cards, the purpose or efficacy of the system is seldom questioned.

It is to the identification and elimination of these and many other causes of poor value that procedure value analysis is devoted. In an organized way, it examines, evaluates, and improves the existing procedure, system, or practice—or it develops a new procedure, system, or practice using value engineering techniques. The value engineering job plan applies the guidelines for the organized approach. Procedure value analysis consists of an information phase, a creative phase, an evaluation phase, an investigation phase, and a reporting phase.

Within these phases the value engineering technique of blast-create-refine is used as the principal technique of analysis.

THE PROCEDURE FLOW CHART

During the information phase a graphic representation is developed of the system or procedure selected for study, using a procedure flow chart. This chart is designed to portray the relationships of the discrete operations and the interrelationship of paperwork with these operations.

There is no single right way to prepare a procedure flow chart. Whatever method affords the optimum visualization to the procedure analyst, to the study team, or to a representative audience is the most beneficial. The level of detail desired in the chart is a very important consideration and requires the individual judgment of the chart maker. A level that depicts minute, insignificant elements of an operation will quickly bore any audience and may result in a chart so complex that it defies comprehension and analysis. Conversely, one that contains inadequate specifics or is too brief may hamper change because of inadequate investigation. A relatively simple procedure can be portrayed graphically on a single sheet of paper, or it can be expanded to cover the walls of a conference room. For example, the procedure for removing beard stubble in the morning can be portrayed with one symbol—the word "shave." It can also be depicted by a series of symbols and words signifying such detailed steps as washing face, gathering equipment, and applying lather. If the purpose is to improve the shaving procedure or to teach someone to shave, the latter chart would be justified. But if the purpose is to chart early morning activities, the former presentation would be adequate. The detail in the chart must be related to the purpose of the chart.

The visualization provided by the procedure flow chart establishes a tangible basis for evaluation and emphasizes cost and time expended. Although the chart should be designed to accommodate the variables involved in a particular study, there are generally accepted guidelines and symbols that have withstood the test of time. The symbols identify the type of operations graphically and facilitate a better and quicker understanding of the procedure. In addition, they assist in assigning cost parameters. The symbols shown in Exhibit 4 are a combination of the standard symbols of the American Society of Mechanical Engineers with modifications devised by the Standard Register Company.

CHART CONSTRUCTION

After the specific parameters of the study have been established, the chart is developed by drawing the symbol for the first element of

Exhibit 21

PROCESSING A FOUR-PART TRAVEL ORDER

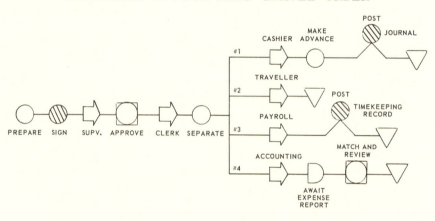

the procedure at the left side of the chart paper. To this symbol is added a brief verbal description of the element, if necessary. The next chronological element is placed to the right of the first symbol and a line is drawn connecting the two. If the second or any subsequent element is performed simultaneously with other elements, the chart expands like a game of dominoes. The example shown in Exhibit 21 is the partial procedure flow chart for processing a four-part form.

Symbols are added to the chart in chronological order and are joined with lines to indicate flow, moving from left to right. The beginner will probably make several adjustments or new charts in his initial attempts, but as experience is gained the chart maker will be able to visualize the chart before constructing it, thereby minimizing second efforts.

In addition to the basic chart construction guides, several refinements are available to the perfectionist. Some of these may be useful; many are redundant. The refinements may be obtained from any book on work simplification techniques or in a one-semester college course on flow charting.

Care should be exercised in adding clarifying verbal descriptions. Many charts duplicate the symbol meaning in the verbal description. The chart itself may be constructed on one of many commercial forms available, although any type of blank paper is adequate. The physical specifications are entirely dependent upon the complexity of the procedure being studied and the skill of the person constructing the chart. For presentations or for team studies, the use of wall charts to increase visualization is recommended—almost required. The visualization is the thing.

Collecting the data from which the chart will be assembled is a critical phase of the study. Since all subsequent study action is based on these data, they must be accurate. The usual tendency is to remain comfortably seated, using the telephone and checking written material to compile the data. This method seldom produces satisfactory results. The procedure flow chart that is based on data collected in this manner will depict the process in terms of what should be done, which will vary considerably from what is being done.

Collecting the data correctly can be tedious and time consuming and can't be accomplished from afar. The investigator must follow each step, relying on personal observations rather than on hearsay or on written procedures. Each worker involved with the study should be interviewed for his description of his actions pertaining to the procedure. Only in this way can the validity of the subsequent chart be assured.

If the study is to be a team effort, the investigation workload can be divided up and each team member can be assigned one area to examine. In addition to facilitating the data-collection task, this method allows for assigning an expert to each part of the procedure. This extra knowledge is important in later phases of the study when the in-depth data that do not appear on the flow chart are required for determining the merit of alternate methods.

Usually the first step in developing a procedure flow chart is the preparation of a chronological verbal listing of the discrete operations involved. When the listing is complete it is transferred, step by step, for graphic presentation on the chart. Each step is identified by type, and the corresponding symbol is placed on the chart. If additional codes or verbal descriptions are required for clarity, they can be inserted inside, below, or above the symbol depending upon the format. Some procedures, because of their simplicity, can be charted directly without including the verbal listing if the analyst is thoroughly knowledgeable in each step of the procedure. It must be remembered, however, that the usefulness of the listing decreases as the level of detail decreases. Until the analyst becomes experienced in the charting techniques, therefore, the listing of procedural steps is strongly recommended.

The following partial listing describes the processing of an employee suggestion (ES) within the group charged with that specific responsibility.

1. Clerk receives ES in mail.
2. Clerk stamps ES with date received.
3. Clerk sends ES to leadman.
4. Leadman assigns ES to a specific analyst.
5. Leadman returns ES to clerk.
6. Clerk serializes ES.
7. Clerk records ES in receipt log.
8. Clerk makes four copies of ES.
9. Clerk stamps No. 2 copy for submitter.
10. Clerk sends No. 2 copy to submitter.
11. Clerk assembles all No. 1 copies.
12. Clerk sends No. 1 copies to Analyst No. 1.
13. Analyst No. 1 reviews for duplication.
14. Analyst No. 1 sends ES's to Analyst No. 2.
15. Analyst No. 2 reviews for duplication.
16. Analyst No. 2 sends ES's to Analyst No. 3.
17. Analyst No. 3 reviews for duplication.
18. Analyst No. 3 sends ES's to clerk.
19. Clerk files ES's in Alpha file.

20. Clerk sends copies No. 3 and No. 4 to analyst.
21. Analyst prepares follow-up record.
22. Analyst prepares an average of two inquiry sheets.

Each processing step starting with Step No. 1 is assigned a symbol indicating its type, and the chart is developed by connecting the symbols in a chronological pattern as shown in Exhibit 22. This is one of many methods that can be used in procedure flow charting. The procedure, when completely charted, serves as the baseline of the existing system against which analytical techniques can be applied.

CHART ANALYSIS

The analysis of a procedure flow chart uses the value engineering technique of the job plan as a guideline to guarantee a systematic and organized analysis. Within the five phases of the job plan, another value engineering technique called *blast-create-refine* is employed as the prime analytical device.

Information phase. During the information phase of the job plan, the first element of the blast-create-refine technique is exercised by blasting down the procedure to its basic function. This is generally accomplished by the same process that is used to determine the basic function of an organization, as described in Chapter 6. The basic function explains the purpose of the procedure and answers the question, What does it do? Care must be exercised to insure that the basic function selected is, in fact, the basic function of the organization involved in the procedure, not of the program supported by the procedure. In the example just given for processing employee suggestions, the analyst could erroneously list the basic function of the employee suggestion *group*, the employee suggestion *program*, or the employee *suggestion* itself. By extending beyond the charted procedure to these other aspects of employee suggestions, the validity of the selected functional definition is jeopardized. The basic function of the employee suggestion processing procedure was initially determined to be *process suggestions*, and a ladder of abstraction was developed to insure that the selected function was indeed the one that best described the purpose of the procedure. (See Exhibit 23.)

After reviewing the levels of abstraction of the previously selected

Exhibit 22

EMPLOYEE SUGGESTION PROCESSING

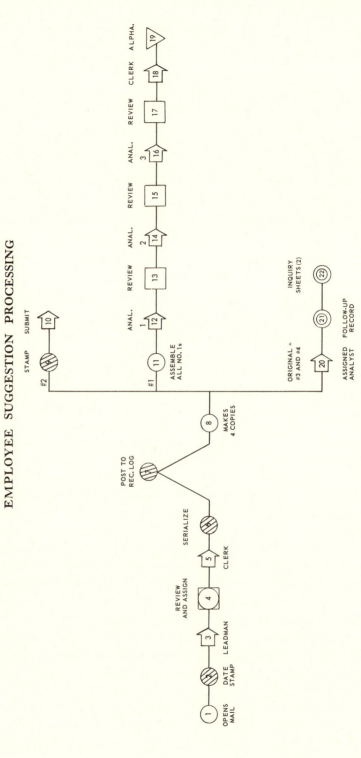

Exhibit 23

LADDER OF ABSTRACTION: EMPLOYEE SUGGESTION
PROCESSING

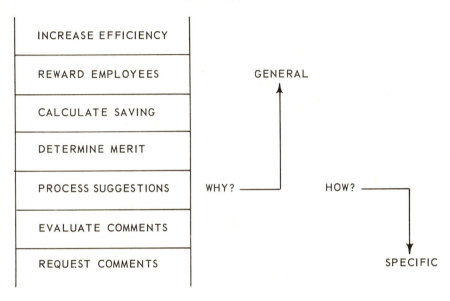

basic function, it was determined that the next higher level, determine merit, was the functional definition that best described the purpose of the procedure for this particular study. It was the one function that would have to remain even though everything else was eliminated.

Creative phase. The creative phase is initiated by developing alternate methods that could be used to satisfy the basic function of the charted procedure. This phase also coincides with the second element of the blast-create-refine technique. The alternates, regardless of practicality, should be recorded on a blackboard, flip chart, or whatever to stimulate the creativity session in developing additional ideas. Judgment of the listed alternates is suspended until all of them have been recorded.

In the employee suggestion procedure, the other methods that could be used to decide merit include having each suggestion reviewed and evaluated by—

1. The industrial engineer.
2. The line supervisor.

3. The employee suggestion analyst.
4. The employee suggestion analyst's telephone inquiries.
5. A committee.

Although this is only a partial listing and not a particularly dramatic one, it typifies the average procedure.

The outcome of the study is directly dependent on the amount of effort expended in the creative phase. If the quantity of alternates developed is relatively small, or if the creativity session is conducted in a perfunctory manner, the resultant changes to the procedure will usually be insignificant. Procedure value analysis studies that fail to accomplish substantial results are generally those in which either the creative phase has been underemphasized or the basic function has been chosen hastily and incorrectly.

Evaluation phase. The judgment of the alternates, suspended during the creative phase, is exercised during the evaluation phase. Each recorded alternate is evaluated for practicality, possibility of implementation, general acceptance, potential cost, potential saving, and so forth, but not in a negative manner. A multitude of reasons can always be developed for rejecting each proposal, but restraint must be imposed during the evaluation phase in questioning the merits of the suggestions. Instead of devising reasons to explain why an idea isn't acceptable, the challenger should take a positive approach and try to uncover methods, additional features, or revisions that might transform an unacceptable procedure into one with a potential for cost saving. As each alternate is evaluated decisions on merit are made. Those that are adjudged unfeasible are culled from the list, leaving those that have potential and a probability of implementation.

During the evaluation phase there is a tendency for the evaluator to select the first seemingly good alternate that appears on the list and to declare further evaluation unnecessary. This snap judgment can doom many studies; even though the selection is indeed the best in all aspects, later developments can prevent implementation. Rather than return to the evaluation phase, the evaluator is prone to decide that the existing procedure isn't bad after all—and a future roadblock is created. For these reasons, all proposals must be evaluated before selection of the "best" one is made.

The evaluation phase is conducted in progressive stages, each stage more detailed than the one before it. The choices that have potential are further screened for detailed cost comparisons and other evaluations. As the screen mesh becomes finer, fewer suggestions are retained until eventually the one best alternate remains. This becomes the cornerstone of the new procedure.

Investigation phase. The final element of the blast-create-refine technique is introduced during the investigation phase. The alternate selected during the evaluation phase is supplemented by the identification and functional definition of the secondary functions—that is, those that add features required to satisfy the basic function. When the secondary functions have been defined, the creativity phase is

Exhibit 24

BASIC FUNCTION AND ALTERNATES

BASIC FUNCTION

ALTERNATES

DECIDE MERIT

1. Industrial engineering evaluation.

2. Line supervision evaluation.

3. Analyst observation.

4. Analyst telephone inquiries.

5. Committee action.

reentered and alternates are developed for each, as was done for the basic function. The alternates are evaluated and the best is selected for each. The basic function's best alternate coupled with the best alternates developed for the secondary functions constitute the skeleton of the new procedure.

In the example of the procedure to process employee suggestions, the procedure flow chart of the existing method was blasted down to the basic function of deciding merit and the new procedure took form with that symbol. (See Exhibit 24.) The buildup progressed with the addition of the secondary functions and the alternate methods to accomplish them, as shown in Exhibit 25.

After the best proposals have been selected, the refinement begins. Specific features or refinements are added to the basic and secondary function alternates to make them acceptable. Increments of function

Exhibit 25

BASIC AND SECONDARY FUNCTIONS WITH ALTERNATES

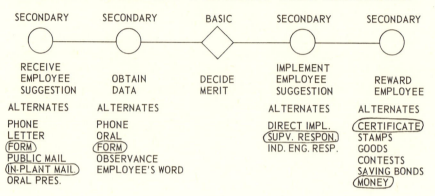

together with increments of cost are added until the refined procedure fully accomplishes the total function. At this point development ceases and the information can be transferred to a procedure flow chart or the proposed procedure can be prepared.

Reporting phase. After the new procedure has been developed, the creative part is over. To realize the full benefits, the proposed procedure must then be implemented and the reporting phase becomes extremely important. Many studies, both value engineering and VAMP, have failed to achieve savings simply because the reporting phase was omitted or deemphasized. The reporting phase is anticlimactic, requires work, and contains relatively little flair compared to previous phases. For these reasons it is often slighted.

The reporting phase has three main objectives:

1. To document the team's effort, thus providing another example of success.
2. To aid in gaining approval from others for the implementation of the proposed procedure.
3. To provide a training aid during the implementation of the proposed procedure.

Of these three objectives, the second is the most important. The implementation of many proposed procedures requires the acceptance, approval, and action of others. These others may be higher-level executives whose approval is necessary or managers who will be affected in some way by the proposed procedure. They must be sold on the merits of the proposal, and the salesmanship is planned during the reporting phase.

The first step is to identify the individuals whose approval must be gained. Their positions within management and their familiarity with the existing procedure should be carefully considered. The second step is to develop a report or presentation that will not only convince these individuals that the proposal should be accepted but will also motivate them toward implementing it. In addition, the benefits of procedure value analysis should be cited.

To be effective, the report should contain the following basic features.

1. *A wall-size procedure flow chart of the existing procedure.* This should be in sufficient depth and of sufficient clarity to insure understanding by the audience. In some cases the chart prepared earlier may be used if it is clear enough. If the report is oral, the chart should be designed with a minimum amount of verbal description and should be used more as a supplementary visual aid. However, it should retain the same number of operations that appeared on the original procedure flow chart to highlight graphically the complexity of a seemingly simple procedure. If the report is written, additional verbal descriptions may be required to convey the meaning.

2. *A cost estimate of the existing procedure.* This estimate can be expressed in dollars, in hours, or (if data are not available) in the quantity of each type of transaction—for example, 50 operations, 30 inspections, 25 transportations.

3. *An identification of the basic and secondary functions.* These can be marked on the wall chart in red or can otherwise be highlighted to display the quantity of operations now being performed to satisfy these functions.

4. *A wall-size procedure flow chart of the proposed procedure.* The chart should contain the same detail that appears on the chart for the existing procedure. The tendency to dramatize results by combining operations that are separate on the existing procedure flow chart should be discouraged, for this action when detected will arouse criticism and will throw suspicion on the entire study.

5. *A cost estimate of the proposed system.* The same cost terms that were used on the existing procedure flow chart should be used here.

6. *A listing of the advantages of the proposed procedure over the existing procedure.* This listing should include not only the cost comparison but also all other tangible and intangible benefits that could result.

7. *An estimate of the probable implementation cost.* The estimate should include such items as the purchase of new equipment, facility changes, and personnel changes.

8. *An implementation program plan.* This should contain a step-by-step procedure of the actions planned to implement the proposal, a time schedule for implementation, and the assignment of specific individuals to perform the actions cited. This plan should be in sufficient detail and in logical sequence so that it will gain approval from the individuals whose concurrence is required. The best program plan is one that motivates the approving authority to direct implementation of the proposal at the end of the presentation.

The steps used in procedure value analysis are so interdependent that the neglect of one will usually make success impossible. If the information phase is slighted, the alternates developed may not satisfy the essential function of the procedure. A lack of emphasis on the creative phase will limit the potential saving. A cursory evaluation of alternatives may lead to a less-than-optimum proposal. A hastily conducted investigation phase can result in an impractical proposal. And an incomplete reporting phase can induce cynicism, leading to a total failure of the study.

9

Benefits of Procedure
Value Analysis

The opportunities that exist for the successful application of procedure value analysis exceed those of organization value analysis because there are so many more procedures than there are organizations. Each organization generally has a multitude of procedures and everyone is familiar with the term procedures manual. Between the covers of the procedures manual lies a fertile field for cost reduction. In addition to the formalized written procedures, such as those authorized by the company president, are a host of departmental or functional procedures. Some are written, others have grown through tradition. Both types represent considerable cost and potential savings. However, the potential can be realized only *after* the procedure has been revised or eliminated. The likelihood of success is substantially enhanced by the proper selection of a study subject.

Selecting a Procedure

Selecting a procedure for value analysis requires almost as much care and planning as selecting an organization for value analysis. In both, the odds for implementation must be weighed seriously and judiciously. The basic criteria for choosing a procedure for study are twofold:

1. The procedure should have a high ratio of potential cost reduction to analysis time.
2. The procedure should lend itself to revision acceptance; that is, it should not contain any apparent significant political or emotional roadblocks to change.

Within these parameters additional criteria can be applied to increase the potential for success by stipulating the sources that can be used to identify high-cost procedures and the areas where these procedures traditionally reside. The following are some of the areas vulnerable to high-cost procedures.

1. *Bottleneck jobs.* Procedures that seem to have as a purpose the harassment of the employee and the advancement of complexity may entail unnecessary costs or may even be the cause of the bottleneck. These procedures are often found in control functions, and they often involve the preparation of a multicopy form.

2. *Time-consuming jobs.* A procedure that requires several pages of detailed instruction to permit a bare understanding and cannot be explained more simply may be riddled with redundant operations. This type of procedure can be found throughout an organization and can thrive in any industrial climate.

3. *Multiple operations.* A procedure that contains a multitude of actions to attain a seemingly simple goal can hide many superfluous costs. An example would be a form, report, or record that requires many successive levels of authorization or approval prior to execution.

4. *Heavy organizational involvement.* Some procedures involve the efforts of many organizations to attain a relatively minor objec-

tive. These situations where the end does not appear to justify the means offer many study subjects.

5. *Long-lived procedures.* A procedure that has been in existence for a long time offers exceptional potential for cost reduction with the potential increasing in proportion to the age of the procedure. An excellent example is a Bureau of Customs form that requires a listing of the number of guns mounted on a merchant vessel prior to entry or clearance of that vessel at U.S. ports. The form was designed in 1790 and is still in use today.

6. *Temporary conditions.* It has been said that nothing is more permanent than a temporary procedure. Procedures developed to provide for temporary conditions often are not revised when the conditions change, and the practice directed by the procedure continues to be a source of expense.

7. *High-cost personnel.* The cost of routine clerical tasks can be greatly increased by assigning them to highly paid professionals. Many companies waste money and talent and cause morale problems as well when they try to give increased importance to a report or procedure by assigning a high-level employee to prepare it. In addition to the cost of preparation, the cost of the recipients' time in reading the report must be considered in establishing total cost. Since the report is prepared on a relatively high level, the distribution list usually contains names of employees on a similar or higher level. Reports or procedures of this nature usually have a high cost-to-function ratio and offer substantial cost-reduction opportunities.

8. *Chronic irritants.* A procedure that often evokes charges of unnecessary red tape by its users can be subjected to procedure value analysis with excellent chances for success. The study of a chronically annoying procedure is especially well suited to a seminar workshop because of the support that will be forthcoming from all parties concerned. Proposals for improvement will be enthusiastically received and promptly implemented.

9. *Few "do" operations.* All procedures involve three basic operations—prepare or make ready, do, and clean up or put away. The only productive one is the *do* operation. A procedure that has many operations, few of which are of the *do* variety, is indicative of high cost and low value and should afford a favorable subject for improvement.

10. *Standard forms.* Standard forms furnish a potential for cost

reduction. The cost of the form and the time required to prepare it are relatively insignificant compared to the cost of the action that may be initiated. A simple form can stimulate the creation of many other records, forms, and reports. The total cost of issuing a standard form can be compared to an iceberg of which only 10 percent is visible. The following are some clues to high-cost, low-value forms:

   a. A form that is prepared with many copies. Each copy usually finds its way to a different organization and generates additional cost in those areas.
   b. An organization that initiates many forms. It is always suspect because of its ability to generate work.
   c. A form containing a voluminous amount of data. The collection of these data can involve many man-hours; if these data are not informative to the recipient, the value is questionable.
   d. Forms that are used extensively, such as personnel forms, payroll forms, purchasing forms, and quality control forms. They are potential sources of savings because of the significant cost they represent.
   e. Many forms that contain similar data. They may be causing duplication of effort and confusion.

In selecting a project for a procedure value analysis study, the experience and attitude of the analyst may help in pinpointing many procedures that seem to represent poor value. His personal involvement, although it may retard purely objective analysis, does provide additional motivation and perseverance so necessary to a successful study. The trade-off is usually desirable.

In the absence of intuitive project identification, many data sources are available within the typical industrial organization that can be used to assist in identifying a proper study project. The following is only a partial listing of these sources.

1. The procedures manual is an excellent source of information. A cursory perusal will uncover many procedures of questionable value, even though the actual practice does not always conform to the specifics of the procedure.

2. A record-controls or records-management group may be able to supply a host of suggested high-cost procedures, reports, and

forms. A record of the cost, usage, or distribution is usually available for review.

3. Contractual reports can be a source of cost reduction primarily because their value is seldom questioned. The fact that a report or procedure is mentioned or alluded to in a contract is sufficient to guarantee immunity. Contractual reports are a source of special interest to a company that has negotiated value engineering incentive clauses in its contract. Although usually restricted to government prime contractors and their subcontractors, the principles of this device are applicable to any venture designed for profit. Briefly, this clause allows the contractor to share a saving with his customer at a negotiated sharing rate if the proposed cost reduction cuts the total cost of the contract and if the implementation requires a revision to the contract. This gives the contractor the incentive to seek ways of reducing the contract cost and also provides the customer with the incentive to accept the proposed revisions. In the absence of a value engineering incentive clause the contractor can benefit by fulfilling the contract stipulations in a less expensive manner.

4. Many companies have established a centralized forms-control organization to evaluate the need for proposed standard forms and to forestall the introduction of redundant and unnecessary forms. Although established with an honorable objective, many such organizations are reduced to forms design and data collection. The control element is often sabotaged by well-meaning employees whose explanations of form needs are incomprehensible to the forms-control personnel. The result is the issuance of new standard form numbers and increased costs. The control aspect is maintained in name only. Nonetheless, this organization can supply data that are extremely useful in identifying procedure value analysis study projects. Information such as the quantity of a specific form used, the quantity of data required to prepare and process a form, the number of forms originated in a particular organization, or the number of forms associated with the same function can provide clues to expensive procedures of dubious value. In addition, the personnel in these areas may be more than willing to identify what they believe to be low-value forms.

5. An organization charged with responsibility for designing paperwork systems and initiating procedures can be the source of many worthwhile study projects. The analysts in these organizations are

acutely aware of complex procedures, and they have access to the background history of these procedures. In addition, since new procedures are developed in this organization, opportunities to avoid costs by applying procedure value analysis in the design phase can be exploited. The avoidance of future costs is a far more important concept than the reduction of existing costs.

One roadblock that might be encountered in this type of organization is similar to one met continually by value engineers practicing in a design section. The proposal to increase the value of a system, a procedure, or a piece of hardware carries implicit criticism of the original designer. The design engineer and the systems and procedures analyst feel they have designed the best system possible within the constraints present at the time of design. The intention of the VAMP specialist to improve on their creation may generate an uncooperative attitude. For these reasons it is recommended that a great deal of tact and empathy be employed in approaching an organization of this nature for study prospects.

6. The computer can conceal many high-cost, low-value procedures and reports. This is due partly to the specialized training apparently required to evaluate the worth of these procedures and reports and partly to the common belief that anything that is a product of punched cards, tapes, or discs must per se be of value. In addition, there is a popular fallacy that computer-generated reports and procedures do *not* incur costs. Computer programmers and systems analysts recognize this fallacy for what it is and are in a strategic position to suggest projects. Many worthwhile proposals for transferring manual tasks to EDP are denied because the total computer capacity is being utilized for reports and procedures some of which are of questionable value. Subjecting a computer-generated report or procedure to procedure value analysis can therefore have the additional benefit of freeing the computer of unnecessary workloads.

The Approach

Procedure value analysis can be performed by an individual or by team action. Each has merit, depending on the circumstances. Normally a team is preferable to an individual if the team members selected have a definite stake in the outcome of the study. Ideally, the procedure chosen for study involves the efforts of four or five organization elements with each element represented on the team. The representatives should be individuals of sufficient management stature to approve subsequent revisions for their specific organizations. The team composition mandates involvement and supplies additional incentive for procedure improvement. Such a team can save many hours in the investigative task, if each member is knowledgeable about the effects of the procedure in his area of responsibility. This same knowledge is particularly useful during the evaluation phase of the study in determining the practicality of the suggestions.

The validity of a procedure value analysis study can depend heavily on the amount of objectivity employed during the study, and the team approach offers benefits in this area. Although each team member is naturally biased in evaluating *his* organization's performance, he is surprisingly objective when evaluating the effectiveness of other areas. In a study with a five-man team, objectivity of 80 percent can be expected. All aspects of the job plan can be more effectively covered by the team approach, and many common roadblocks to implementation can be circumvented.

The most important advantage of the team approach is that it increases the probability of implementation. And the fact that each member of the team can authorize implementation of any study proposals in his organization almost guarantees an actual saving. Implementing a proposal that results in a modest saving is far more important than publishing proposed dramatic savings that are never achieved.

Because of circumstances, the individual approach to procedure value analysis may be necessary. The time and effort that must be spent in selecting a team and then in keeping it together is substantial, and conditions may render a team approach unfeasible. Usually the type of individuals desired for a team study have more tasks to complete than they have time to complete them. To add to their workloads and also secure their full cooperation requires the skill of a professional diplomat. In addition, an excess of volunteers is not usually a problem in new VAMP programs. Often the team members must be appointed and directed to participate by their superiors. In the absence of motivational stimuli, the individual study approach may be the only answer.

The individual approach to procedure value analysis is not without merit. One advantage is the lack of embarrassment that is sometimes associated with a team study. When a major management deficiency is uncovered during a team study, the deficiency is evident to at least the team members. If the deficiency is the responsibility of one member of the team, some embarrassment may ensue. It may also be necessary to emphasize the blunder on the procedure flow chart for presentation to higher management, which may deepen the embarrassment. If the procedure being analyzed was originally developed by one individual and imposed on others, dramatic improvements can reflect on the originator's managerial ability. This is illogical, because *any* job can be improved, yet the attitude persists. On the other hand, the individual approach will result in the originator's improving his own creation, which is always considered good and virtuous. This obvious desire constantly to improve his own output will further his managerial reputation within the company.

The individual approach may be the most expeditious where time is a critical factor. The individual can pace his own efforts and provide a flexible study schedule. The team approach is often subject to interruptions which, if not controlled, can destroy the study effort. A study schedule that will suit each team member and yet remain effective is a remote possibility.

The choice between the team study approach and the individual approach demands a careful trade-off of benefits and can be made only at the time and place of the study project selection. Each occurrence introduces a new set of variables.

HUMAN RELATIONS

On the surface it would seem that procedure value analysis should not have to be concerned with aspects of human relations, since the proposed improvements will affect things rather than people. The reduction in the cost of a procedure and the reduction in the number of people in an organization should have different emotional impacts on the employees concerned. However, little perception is required to realize that the cost of a procedure or system basically consists of the hours employees spend in conforming to that procedure or system.

If, as a result of procedure value analysis, a procedure is reduced from 100 operations to 50, the saving is generally calculated in hours. If these hours cannot be identified, segregated, and used for some other effort of value, then the analyst has no assurance that a saving did in fact occur. Even though a procedure has been reduced in size or scope, until the alleged hours saved are disposed of usefully, the claimed savings are savings in name only. Therefore, procedure value analysis can have the same human relations factors as does organization value analysis. But, because of the subtleties of procedure value analysis, the quantity and intensity of these factors are reduced.

When necessary, a procedure value analysis study can be conducted effectively, but the implementation of proposed changes can be jeopardized by neglecting to anticipate the roadblocks. These must be identified early in the study and their impact must be considered during the investigation and reporting phases of the job plan.

Roadblocks are not difficult to create. In fact, most people can set them up with little effort. They are primarily the result of habit or attitudes, and, although the nature of the study will impose roadblocks peculiar to that study, there are three that should be considered in each procedure value analysis.

1. *Authorship.* The existing procedure may have been written or established by an individual whose approval must be gained before revisions can be effected. In this instance, the author's support of the study purposes must be secured early and his involvement during the study is highly desirable. His natural reluctance to admit that something he devised can be improved upon is lessened with tact. Although his inherent subjectivity may somewhat hinder team analysis, his approval of participation in the study can be critical to its success.

2. *Job security.* The impact of job displacement as a result of proposed revision to a procedure must be considered in the reporting phase of the job plan. It should not restrict the proposal, nor should it inhibit the selection of the best alternate, for the objective of the study continues to be the fulfillment of the function at the lowest possible cost. However, awareness of the threat to the job security of the employees involved can assist the team in identifying other roadblocks that will impede study progress and implementation of the proposal. Certainly a supervisor who faces the elimination of all or a significant part of his organization as a result of a study proposal cannot be counted on as an advocate of the proposal. By recognizing this, the team can better anticipate the rationalizations that will be offered in defense of the status quo and can be prepared with adequate rebuttals.

3. *Resistance to change.* Regardless of the merits of a proposed

change in procedure, resistance will be encountered. The procedure has already established comfortable and secure habits of operation, and the proposed revisions threaten these habits. Usually the change will necessitate the development of new habits which are not as comfortable or as secure. This potential roadblock deserves considerable attention during the refining phase of the blast-create-refine technique. If, in developing the proposed procedure, low-cost concessions to old habits can be included, resistance will diminish and support or at least acceptance of the new procedure will be achieved.

STUDY SUBJECT COMPLEXITY

The easiest way to prevent success of a study is to select a complex procedure as a project for a team of neophytes in procedure value analysis. It is disastrous, for the tentacles of a complex procedure will strangle the motivation and initiative of the best-intentioned team as well as supply future roadblocks to procedure value analysis. The team that becomes frustrated by a complex study will usually blame the techniques of procedure value analysis rather than admit its ineptitude in applying these techniques. Future support from the team members cannot be expected; neither will they be indifferent. They will have developed an especially effective roadblock: "I've tried it and it doesn't work." This attitude they pass on to their colleagues.

There is a tendency on the part of the uninitiated to select a project that entails a large expenditure of money so that the study results can provide dramatic evidence of business waste. Where this is allowed to occur, the only waste is usually the time spent by the team before it withdraws from the study. The time required to conduct such a study, even with experienced team members, will usually exceed the estimates developed when the project is selected.

The beginner to procedure value analysis would do well to limit his initial attacks to a simple adversary. A relatively uncomplicated common form will provide sufficient challenge, and as experience is gained the scope can be extended gradually.

When procedure value analysis is introduced, the focus should be on training as many members of management as time and money permit and not on the immediate resolution of all the company's problems. Once a sufficient number of managers have been trained, they can band together to tackle the complexities of large organizations and sprawling procedures.

BENEFITS OF PROCEDURE VALUE ANALYSIS

The primary benefit to be gained from procedure value analysis is a significant reduction in a procedure's cost while maintaining or increasing its value. Although this benefit alone is more than sufficient justification for using procedure value analysis, it also has many valuable side effects which can equal the achievement of cost savings in importance. Five of these corollary benefits are discussed in the following pages.

1. *Cost sensitivity*. Procedure value analysis studies promote a cost-sensitive attitude in the practitioners of the techniques and also in those affected by the study. Cost sensitivity differs from the overused terms *cost-conscious attitude* and *cost awareness* in that these terms do not imply corrective action. An employee can be well aware of excessive or unnecessary costs without ever questioning the value that these costs represent. An employee who is sensitive to costs will as a rule challenge those he considers improper. Although this differentiation may seem pedantic, *cost sensitivity* better describes the attitude desired.

As the use of this discipline spreads throughout the company, the trained managers begin to think of function as the criterion of value. This changed mode of thinking will not be restricted to procedures or organizations but will permeate each element of the business. The marketing effort will automatically be evaluated on the basis of function and cost as well as manufacturing schedules, hardware products, and accounting features. The functional approach teaches the manager to be wary and critical of attempts to define plans and objectives in unmeasurable abstractions. This attitude of cost sensitivity will restrain the establishment of wasteful procedures in the future because the trained manager will construct the new procedures on the basis of the function-to-cost ratio. In the utopian state, maximum sensitivity would eliminate the need for procedure value analysis.

2. *Cost visibility*. The identification of costs is the most important aspect of cost reduction, value engineering, and, for that matter, any function of business. Indeed, the review of costs often occupies a

considerable portion of the typical manager's time. The cost of hardware is estimated and reviewed, and the cost of equipment is reviewed. In addition, several organizations are established to estimate, control, and reduce costs. But the costs that are estimated, controlled, and reduced are for the most part hardware costs to which an arbitrary percentage is added to provide for everything else. Seldom does a manager reflect on the cost of a procedure. The reason is that no one has informed him of these costs and they go unnoticed and unquestioned. Yet they constitute a large segment of total cost.

The techniques of procedure value analysis assist in establishing costs associated with procedures by breaking down the elements of a procedure and assigning each element a time estimate. These estimates provide the manager with a comparison tool and a guideline which he can use to estimate the cost of other procedures. This aspect of procedure value analysis can result in the avoidance of significant future costs.

3. *Management communication.* The lack of communication in business has been the scapegoat for many business deficiencies and managerial blunders. It has been the topic of numerous articles in business periodicals and a great many books as well. Indeed, if one were to rely implicitly on the admonitions and suggestions of the communication experts, he would discover that all business problems would be resolved if he could learn to communicate more effectively. The substance of what he has to communicate seems to be of little significance.

The problem in business communication is that the manager, in the comfort and security of his own office, just won't take the time and expend the physical effort to communicate with others. The problem isn't semantics; it's complacency, or the desire for noninvolvement. Procedure value analysis forces involvement and opens new lines of communication. As each team member collects the information he needs to prepare his portion of the procedure flow chart he is usually exposed to many organizational elements, and, if he is to collect reliable data, he must talk to the supervisors and managers of these areas. This exchange generally develops a rapport between the investigator and those whom he is investigating that remains long after the study comes to an end.

The use of procedure value analysis to open lines of management communication enlarges the team member's knowledge of company operations and, in turn, furnishes the company with a more versatile and effective manager.

4. *Managerial morale.* Many companies have introduced a spirit of competitiveness so severe that each department regards the others as little competitive companies. Mild competition in business is useful, but fierce competition as the basis for informal departmental objectives promotes lack of cooperation and subversive actions. The loser in such a contest is the company. Situations often occur where department managers engaged in this kind of competition become so estranged that they refuse to communicate with each other except by formal memos. In these instances the company managerial morale has faltered.

Procedure value analysis can have a refreshing effect on managerial morale by bringing dissident managers together in a team study. During the study the men are engaged in a concerted effort to attain a common goal, and the individual desire for achievement can create a cooperative attitude that has lasting beneficial effects. In the performance of the study the team members must talk to each other, and usually any animosities present at the beginning of the study dissolve quickly. The creation of a management team that will work efficiently and without conflict to attain company objectives is a universal business goal. Applying the principles of procedure value analysis throughout the company can initiate, further, or achieve fulfillment of this goal.

5. *Training device.* When a procedure value analysis study results in a drastic revision to a procedure, the individuals involved with the revised procedure must be trained in the new methods. The procedure flow charts of both the old and the new methods can be used as excellent training aids to reduce changeover costs. These charts are also useful in orienting new employees quickly. In addition, the study itself has inherent training qualities, especially when a new or recently reassigned manager participates as a team member. In analyzing a procedure relating to his assigned area of responsibility, the new manager is afforded the opportunity to explore associated areas and to gain a better understanding and overview of his own function. This training can partially circumvent the normal, costly orientation period.

*   *   *

The techniques of procedure value analysis are logical and not too difficult to understand, but sometimes the initial application can be disappointing if the procedure projects are selected at random. The discipline is not automatic. It requires a good deal of judgment on the part of the surveyor, and his ability to discern the optimum conditions of application will be reflected in the study results.

The strategy planning involved in the first attempts to conduct a study should not be treated lightly, and selecting conditions that improve the probability of success is not at all unbusinesslike. The guidelines provided in this chapter establish the minimum criteria for project selection and highlight areas susceptible to high-cost procedures. Some of the best sources of project selection data available in an industrial organization are mentioned as aids in proper procedure selection. The team approach to a study usually affords more benefits than the individual approach and can reduce significant but often overlooked roadblocks to implementation.

The benefits that can be gleaned from procedure value analysis are far reaching and sometimes surpass the cost-reduction objectives in importance. These corollary effects achieve the purpose of many other management programs to upgrade managerial effectiveness.

Procedure value analysis is a new and unique approach to combating the paperwork problem. If sufficient time and effort are invested in the process and if each phase of the job plan is exploited, the return on investment will substantially exceed the return usually realized in the application of ordinary cost-reduction efforts.

IO

VAMP Training

A COMPLETE understanding of the techniques and principles of VAMP can be achieved without inordinate effort. Course prerequisites or specialized backgrounds are not required and the jargon is minimal. Unfortunately, understanding by itself is insufficient for successful application. Training is mandatory. The method and duration of the training will be dependent upon several variables, such as the training staff available, the training facilities available, and the number of supervisors to be trained. Since these variables can differ significantly from case to case, any attempt to develop an ideal training plan for all possible conditions would be futile. Instead, the merits of different training methods will be discussed; the choice of method must depend on individual needs.

LECTURE AND CONFERENCE

There are many instances where the lecture or the lecture-and-conference method can be used beneficially, but seldom do these methods provide the recipients with the knowledge for effective application. A lecture or a series of lectures may be of value as an introduction to a formal training program. Because lectures can reach a large audience, all managers can be informed of the basic tenets of VAMP. This prelude may increase the degree of future cooperation and endorsement during actual studies, and the time expended by each manager in listening is relatively small. Since the encroachment on the manager's time is minimal, his attendance at the lecture is almost assured and his attitude will probably be favorable. The lecture as a prime instrument of motivation rather than as an instrument of learning has many advantages.

The effectiveness of the lecture-and-conference or classroom training can be moderately enhanced if sufficient time is allocated for practical examples of VAMP's use. The use of many examples is necessary to offset the lack of actual experience in the human relations aspects of VAMP.

Workshop Seminar

Roger Ascham once said, "Experience teacheth more in one year than learning in twenty, but learning teacheth safely, when experience maketh more miserable than wise."* If this 20-to-1 ratio even approximates reality, neither total experience nor total learning represents optimum value in training. A combination of both is desirable so that the risk associated with experience is reduced and the time required for learning is lessened. This combination can be attained in workshop seminars.

The workshop seminar, combining experience with instruction, has long been used as an effective method to train value engineers. Actual projects, preferably of a high-cost, low-value nature, are employed to lend realism to the training and also to effect savings wherever possible. Since the purpose of the seminar is to train students in the application of VAMP, the corollary saving feature should not be emphasized to the degree of compromising this purpose. The use of actual projects motivates the students much more effectively than using canned examples because the student experiences the merits

* Roger Ascham, *The Schoolmaster*, Cornell University Press, Ithaca, New York, 1967.

of VAMP himself, rather than just hearing about the results accomplished by others. The practical approach creates a far greater stimulus to the future use of VAMP than does the theoretical approach, where the detail advantages are spelled out under optimum conditions. In addition, the student becomes acquainted with the human relation factors so difficult to demonstrate adequately under classroom conditions.

For these reasons, the workshop seminar is recommended as the most effective form of VAMP training.

Training Objectives

The purposes of VAMP training can be expressed in both immediate and long-range training objectives. The immediate objectives, which should be accomplished prior to the end of the seminar, are—

1. To provide the seminar students with sufficient VAMP acumen to enable them to
    a. identify high-cost, low-value projects beyond the scope of the seminar;
    b. organize, participate in, or direct future nonseminar VAMP studies;
    c. participate in future VAMP seminars as project leaders.
2. To increase student motivation in the application of VAMP by overcoming any inherent cynicism.
3. To promote student morale by involving them as team members, and to increase rapport among managers.
4. To increase the student's overall perspective and knowledge of company operations by exposing him to areas other than his own, thereby increasing his value to the company.
5. To develop an attitude of constructive discontent and to increase the student's sensitivity to organization and procedure costs.
6. To effect a cost saving in seminar projects without compromising the quality of instruction.

The long-range training objectives whose importance should not be overlooked are—

1. To provide a pool of managers knowledgeable in VAMP philosophy and trained in VAMP techniques. The higher the organization level trained, the greater the potential for meaningful cost reduction or cost avoidance. But to apply VAMP at these levels requires managers at these levels who are trained in VAMP.

2. To promote the acceptance of VAMP at all organization levels by creating VAMP advocates in the workshop seminars. This will also diminish the effectiveness of roadblocks to future VAMP studies or eliminate them altogether.

3. To maximize the value of the total company organizations and procedures by fostering the functional approach to business.

MANAGEMENT SUPPORT

Almost every management tool, technique, or process introduced during the past decade has been offered with the admonition that the user gain top management support before putting the new device to work. Such recommendations could be viewed as superfluous, for seldom is anything accomplished without top management support. If the company president must personally endorse the initial use of all new management techniques, the company has significant problems whose solution exceeds the scope of VAMP.

Top managers are erudite businessmen who, through education, experience, or intuition, have acquired the ability to discern correctly and to decide quickly. The introduction of VAMP into a company shouldn't need top management support—only the absence of opposition. If managers are to give their active support to a VAMP effort, they *must* be convinced of its value and must judge the merits of VAMP in actual practice. The absence of opposition is sufficient for *initial* efforts. When the results of VAMP have been evaluated, management support will be assured.

There are some actions that can be beneficial in stimulating management interest during the period when VAMP is introduced. The most important of these is the development of an excellent and timely sales effort to provide the setting for acceptance and positive action. This effort should include—

1. The company VAMP training objectives.
2. The need for VAMP training.
3. The cost benefits of VAMP.
4. The corollary benefits of VAMP.
5. The estimated cost of VAMP training and the potential return on investment compared to other company training programs, if the comparative data can be collected.
6. The efforts that other companies within the industry are expending in VAMP training and application.

If the company has a training group or department, its involvement in the sales effort is highly desirable. Such groups usually consist of highly trained educators who can offer significant assistance in developing a training program. It is their business. Also, if they are circumvented they can erect formidable barriers to successful implementation. During this period of VAMP introduction, the proponents will have several opportunities to exercise many of the human relations principles that are included as part of the seminar curriculum.

SEMINAR ORGANIZATION

The curriculum developed for the VAMP workshop seminar requires approximately 40 hours of instruction and student project time. This time requirement can be satisfied in a variety of ways; for example, two hours per day for twenty days, eight hours per day for five days, or four hours per day for ten days. The seminar director will have to determine the schedule that is best suited to company conditions.

Conducting a seminar over an extended period—for example, one month—has definite undesirable effects. Although this may be entirely satisfactory in a college or university curriculum, the scheduling and attendance problems that arise in business detract from the quality of a seminar. On the other hand, conducting the seminar in one week may create equally undesirable effects. The students are from managerial levels of organization and usually cannot (or think they cannot) afford to leave their duties and responsibilities unguarded for an entire week. Since many managers will be included, a one-week seminar in a small company could entail a managerial exodus which would probably create appreciable roadblocks.

Experience has shown that the optimum schedule for a VAMP workshop seminar is four hours per day for ten consecutive working days. These daily periods, which can be scheduled for the morning or afternoon, leave the balance of the day for the VAMP students to carry on with their own work and evaluate the efficiency of, or provide guidance to, the employees they have assigned to fill in for them temporarily. The four-hour seminar periods are long enough to stimulate and sustain the students' interest in the instruction and the controlled project work, and the continuity of the daily sessions adds training coherence and increases the importance of attendance.

The workshop seminar is based on team learning. Each student team should be composed of four or five members, with one member assigned the additional task of team captain. (The method of selecting team members is explained later.) The captain has the responsibility of controlling his team's efforts within the guidelines established by the seminar director. He also acts as spokesman during the presentations of the team's reports of progress on the assigned project. The task of recording the team progress, which often is useful to later seminar students and also provides a case history in support of planned VAMP emphasis, is assigned to a team member by the captain.

In the course of seminar instruction, and particularly during the controlled project work, the teams have a tendency to neglect or ignore some phases of the job plan. Unless restrained, each team will accept the first functional definition offered as the correct or best one, accept the first alternate method developed as the best one, and develop its proposal while thinking the whole process is pretty easy. Through sheer chance or intuition the proposal may be excellent, but the odds do not favor such an occurrence. Even in that rare instance, the team fails to use the newly learned techniques to the full, and the team members' future effectiveness in VAMP application is questionable.

To insure an orderly progression through the phases of the job plan, project leaders are assigned. Each project leader undertakes the surveillance of two teams and has the responsibility of guiding the teams through the various phases of the job plan, thus insuring that each phase is fully exploited. The leader does not assist the team in analyzing the project or in collecting data. The project leaders should be employees who have attended previous VAMP seminars and who have exhibited a high degree of analytical ability and interest in VAMP. The selection of well-trained project leaders can contribute materially to the success of a workshop seminar.

The number of teams that can be accommodated adequately during one workshop seminar depends upon the stage of the training program. Early in the program, or during the first seminar, the number of teams should not ordinarily exceed three. This is because there are no trained employees to assign as project leaders and each instructor has to perform that function along with his other duties. Also, the seminar instructors themselves are relatively inexperienced in VAMP at this point. As the instructors become more adept—or if trained consultants are employed—the number of teams per seminar can be increased. Students of early seminars can then be assigned as project leaders. The practical maximum number of teams for a VAMP workshop seminar is eight. Beyond this point seminar control is difficult to maintain. Through experience it has been found that the ideal seminar consists of six teams.

PROJECT SELECTION

Each team is assigned two projects, one on organization value analysis and one on procedure value analysis. Although the scheduled 40 hours would appear to offer ample time to complete moderately complex projects, in reality it is scarcely sufficient for the adequate treatment of the simplest projects.

The organization value analysis project is selected first. The ideal organization consists of six to ten employees with one supervisor and is engaged in a fairly repetitive task. To insure the cooperation of the organization, a manager interested in VAMP and willing to participate as a seminar student is asked to volunteer one of the elements of his total organization as a subject for study. The manager is then assigned as captain of the team that is using his organization as the project.

When the organization value analysis projects have been identified and the managerial volunteers have been acquired, the procedure value analysis projects are chosen. These should consist of relatively simple forms or procedures, originating in or processed through the organization projects selected and affecting other elements of the organization. A multicopy form that is used extensively and contains just a few items of information, and one that also requires processing by four other organizations in addition to the controlling or originating organization, is well suited for seminar study. The seminar director should be explicit regarding the need for simplicity; otherwise, the team captain will generally select some bottleneck procedure of maximum complexity. Exhibit 26 illustrates the relationship of the organization and procedure projects. Project selections should be completed at least four weeks prior to the scheduled start of the seminar.

STUDENT SELECTION

The choice of students is in part dictated by the project. The team captains in all cases have been selected with the organization value analysis project, and the remaining team members are selected on the basis of their association with the procedure project. Each organizational area affected by the procedure value analysis project should provide a representative as a team member who is of sufficient management stature to approve the implementation of proposed changes for his department.

The team captain is usually acquainted with individual managers in associated areas and can assist in the identification of potential team members. Other criteria, such as a member's age and disposition to change, can be employed. Normally, the ambitious young manager noted for his readiness to accept change may be an excellent seminar prospect; but to expand the VAMP effort the experienced manager's support is also required. The praise and enthusiasm of an experienced manager who previously had exhibited a critical attitude toward VAMP has far more impact on total company attitudes than do accolades from managers who investigate the merits of all new management techniques. A team mixture of young managers with their enthusiasm and initiative and experienced managers with their knowledge of company operations and future propaganda potential is strongly recommended.

The mere identification of team-member prospects doesn't guarantee their attendance at the seminar on opening day. Some may resist this imposition on their time, and gentle persuasion may avail little. Even in those instances when the prospect voluntarily commits himself to the seminar, his attendance may be irregular. He feels that since he committed himself he can rescind the commitment at his conven-

Exhibit 26

PROJECT AND TEAM SELECTION

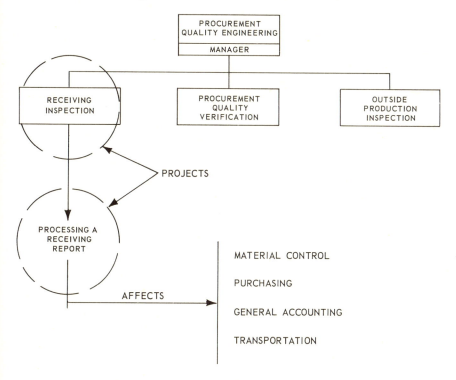

SELECTION

Organization Project — Receiving Inspection
Procedure Project   — Processing Receiving Report

TEAM COMPOSITION —

Team Captain — Manager of procurement quality engineering
Members — Manager of material control
Manager of purchasing
Manager of general accounting
Manager of transportation

ience. For these reasons, it is recommended that the seminar director solicit the support of the prospect's superior to direct his participation.

At least one week prior to the scheduled start of the seminar, each team member should receive a letter of assignment which bears his manager's signature and which specifies who is to replace him for the duration of the seminar. Ideally, personnel selected for VAMP training should be at the highest practical level, and it is advisable that each team member be on the same level.

FACILITIES AND CURRICULUM

The seminar facilities should be planned well ahead of the starting date. The first decision that must be made is whether to conduct the seminar on company premises or at an outside facility. An outside facility has the advantage of being removed from business emergencies that tend to disrupt training sessions by requiring the immediate presence of a team member at a location away from the classroom. On the other hand, much of the team's effort in the project work requires timely access to in-plant data and personnel. Since the need for data outweighs in importance the occasional interruptions, it is recommended that the seminar be conducted on company premises whenever the physical facilities are available.

A meeting room large enough to contain the number of teams scheduled for the seminar should be reserved for the duration. Each team requires one average-size conference table and comfortable chairs. In addition, the room should be well ventilated and relatively free from outside noise. It must have wall space sufficient to display the procedure flow charts and the organization value analysis charts. The instructor's lectern and visual aids should be situated where the students will have maximum visibility. An area should be reserved adjacent to the meeting room to provide for telephones and morning coffee.

Since the students will spend most of the 40 seminar hours in a meeting room, the small amount of planning time required to insure a comfortable atmosphere should not be overlooked.

An example of a typical VAMP workshop seminar curriculum can be found in the Appendix.

TRAINING MATERIALS

The training materials needed in a VAMP workshop seminar are basic and inexpensive. They include:

1. Training Aids
   a. Overhead projector.
   b. Screen.
   c. 16mm movie projector.
   d. Blackboard and chalk.
   e. Flip-chart easel.
2. Student Materials
   a. One three-ring binder per student containing—
      (1) 60 OVAC task data sheets (Exhibit 12).
      (2) 20 OVAC task lists (Exhibit 14).
      (3) 10 OVAC activity lists (Exhibit 11).
      (4) 10 OVAC's (Exhibit 15).
      (5) 25 OVAC analysis sheets (Exhibit 10).
      (6) 20 procedure flow charts, 11″ × 17″.
      (7) 1 set of practice examples.
      (8) 1 procedure flow chart symbol template.
   b. Two OVAC wall charts per team with four extensions.
   c. One roll of wall-size procedure flow chart paper per team.
   d. One large procedure flow chart symbol template per team.
   e. Two marking pens per team, one red and one black.

The quantity of forms specified for the student's notebook is sufficient to satisfy the normal seminar requirements and to allow the student to perform an additional VAMP study in his own area after the seminar has been completed. A supply of forms should be kept available for the students to expand the VAMP studies into several areas. The forms, wall charts, instructor lesson plans, and visual aids are commercially available through the Value Management Institute of La Jolla, 637 Arenas, La Jolla, California.

Training Staff

The ideal seminar staff consists of a training director, a training specialist, an assistant instructor, and one project leader for each two teams. The training director has the overall responsibility for directing and coordinating all aspects of the training program, including the training schedule, facilities planning, student selection, project selection, guest speakers, presentation arrangements, and the follow-up seminar report. He is the person primarily responsible for the success of VAMP training. The training specialist, under the guidance of the training director and with the help of the assistant instructor, conducts the actual training sessions. The duties of the project leaders have already been delineated.

Guest Speakers

As illustrated by the sample curriculum in the Appendix, the moderate use of guest speakers can contribute to the quality of training and can create additional interest on the part of the students. The use of experts also lends prestige to the seminar. Every effort should be made to persuade the company's chief executive to assume the role of keynote speaker for the seminar. Not only will this indicate management interest to the students, but it will also help the chief executive to learn more of the VAMP philosophy.

The lesson on the functional approach calls for a guest speaker unless the training specialist has had considerable experience in teaching this topic. Because of its importance to the seminar, it is recommended that a specialist in the value engineering functional approach be obtained for this lesson. The sessions on human relations and creative thinking also are well suited for guest speakers. These two topics are specialties, and many experts are available as guest speakers.

Speaking invitations should be extended at least two months prior to the beginning of the seminar. Good speakers are likely to have many bookings, and last-minute requests may often be declined.

FOLLOW-UP

The analysis of a project and the subsequent proposals developed during the seminar remain of little dollar value until implemented. Proposals save nothing. In this era of creative management, maximum emphasis and prestige are directed toward the creative thinking abilities of the employee, with little attention given to the undramatic, arduous task of implementation. The erroneous idea prevails that creativity by itself is sufficient; once the creative idea is expressed, innovation occurs automatically. This isn't the way it happens at all. The proposals developed in many value engineering seminars are discarded immediately after the presentation. These projects are presented to management with savings claims of 50 to 100 percent, but in many instances the savings go unclaimed because no one is willing to invest the time and effort required to implement the proposals successfully. Failure to implement seminar projects has a very undesirable effect on the training reputation of a company.

It is the responsibility of the training director to follow up until the seminar projects have been discarded after additional reevaluation or accepted and implemented. When all the projects have been disposed of, a report should be prepared explaining each project from its inception to its disposition. Copies of the follow-up report should be forwarded to the company chief executive and his staff, the team members and their managers, and those attending the final presentations.

MASTER SCHEDULE FOR THE WORKSHOP SEMINAR

The following time schedule represents the optimum planning lead times for completion of the important milestones:

1. *Develop curriculum* ten weeks prior to the seminar starting date. (In a continuing training program, the curriculum should become solidified after three or four seminars.)

2. *Select and invite guest speakers* eight weeks prior to the starting date.
3. *Secure facilities* seven weeks prior to the starting date.
4. *Select OVAC projects and team captains* four weeks prior to the starting date.
5. *Select procedure projects* three weeks prior to the starting date.
6. *Secure training materials* three weeks prior to the starting date.
7. *Start publicity* three weeks prior to the starting date. It should continue until after the seminar is concluded.
8. *Select project leaders* two weeks prior to the starting date.
9. *Select students* two weeks prior to the starting date.
10. *Obtain letters of assignment for students* one week prior to the starting date.
11. *Send out presentation invitations* one week after the seminar begins.
12. *Issue follow-up report* as soon as possible after the disposition of all seminar projects.

TRAINING EVALUATION

Measuring the effectiveness of management training efforts is one of the most difficult tasks in industry. The students' knowledge can be measured to some degree by testing and observation of classroom application, but the students' knowledge per se does not guarantee future use and return on training investment. Training officials can hope that the techniques and philosophies taught in the classrooms are being put to everyday use. But how can the impact of a course in principles of management be measured? How can a change in the managerial ability of a student be measured, and what is the baseline for measurement? A VAMP workshop seminar is not altogether exempt from these gnawing questions, but its effect can be partially measured.

In order to conduct an organization value analysis study, the analyst needs a generous supply of OVAC forms and preliminary forms. The disbursement of these forms assumes they are being used, and the areas of use can be identified. The use of procedure value analysis is more difficult to measure in that special forms are not required to conduct a study. In either case, the future results are not likely to appear as identifiable entries in the monthly profit and loss statements.

The training director should be acutely aware that the potential of VAMP is made manifest not during the seminar but in later use. Accordingly, he should continually seek new means for promoting VAMP philosophy and techniques as well as new methods for evaluating the merit of training.

* * *

The successful application of VAMP within a company hinges on thorough training. The techniques must be acquired through controlled and guided application. The knowledge gained from books and periodicals is important, but the chasm between learning and experience can be bridged most effectively by the workshop seminar. The use of actual projects in the seminar adds a certain flair lacking in typical classroom education and may even result in savings that exceed the cost of the seminar.

The workshop seminar is an excellent method of introducing VAMP to the company as a management experiment. It will offer a challenge to the disbelievers in new techniques and an opportunity to the more progressive managers.

The seminar plays a vital but not an all-encompassing role in VAMP training. It is only part of the overall plan to equip company managers with the capability to increase the value of organizations and procedures and to motivate them to exploit this capability.

II

VAMP in Schools, Hospitals, and Government

T HE prolific growth of paperwork and organization in industry has received considerable attention in recent years, and, as might be expected, the efforts and devices developed to discourage this expansion have been directed primarily toward private industry. Work simplification, value engineering, methods improvement, work measurement, and cost-reduction programs have all been products *of* private industry for application *in* private industry. Although some of these techniques or disciplines have been adopted by governments, both federal and state, their use has generally been sporadic. Occasionally, the Federal Government is attacked for its role in the paperwork plot, and the cries of laxity and wasteful generation of paper increase in intensity as election periods approach. After the votes are tallied, the accusations abate.

For some unknown reason two types of institutions escape critical analysis and evaluation almost entirely—institutions of higher learning and hospitals. In the case of colleges and universities, this immunity may result from the assumption that they are preeminent in all fields and the corollary assumption that they are bound to operate at maximum efficiency. In addition, any increase in the cost of operation can be passed on to the taxpayer or the student in toto.

Hospitals for the most part were founded by men of medicine, not businessmen, and hospital procedures and organizations that operate at less than businesslike efficiency are tolerated as long as the service —medical care—does not deteriorate. As with universities, any increase in cost is borne directly by the consumer. The implication is that neither the university nor the hospital is motivated to cost reduction by profit objectives, competition, or a diminishing demand for its services. Each is basically monopolistic. Seldom can an afflicted person shop around for the best value in hospital room rates. He goes to the hospital that is nearest his home or the one where his doctor is a member of the staff. High school seniors do some university shopping on the basis of their level of competence as students and the income level of their parents. But the great majority of university aspirants are relegated to the position of the selected rather than the selectors. The monopolistic tendencies inherent in these institutions are not conducive to enthusiastic acceptance of cost-cutting programs.

In the past few years the cost of educating a student and the cost of maintaining a hospital patient have spiraled upward, well beyond the economy as a whole and in sharp contrast to the traditional gradual increases. This sudden rise in costs has caused alarm among administrators of these institutions, and efforts to reduce costs have been introduced either by the institutions themselves or by outside agencies responsible for controlling the expenditures. Unfortunately, many of these efforts result from a demand to reduce the budget by an arbitrary percentage. This figure, developed by statistical whim, is totally unrelated to the value of the services being performed and in effect penalizes the efficient administrator who has attained a high function-to-cost ratio. As a result of this unrealistic method of cost reduction, many services have been curtailed, with a loss of value far greater than the decrease in spending.

There is a definite need for VAMP in these institutions to insure a reduction of cost *without* a commensurate decrease in the value of services.

UNIVERSITIES

The state university versus the state legislature is not an uncommon contest in the United States today, and a detailed description of the day-to-day charges and countercharges occupies a portion of many daily newspapers. The legislature usually insists that the enormous expenditures of the universities be controlled, while the public relations officers of the universities counter by accusing the legislature of undermining the entire educational system of the state. These annual contests usually terminate in a standoff.

If educational planning and funding were left entirely in the hands of educators, the country could become one giant university offering perpetual education. If legislatures had full reign, all constituents would be afforded the finest education at no cost to the students or to the taxpayers. Indeed, if the university could also produce a small annual profit, the legislature would be satisfied. The answer obviously is somewhere between the two extremes, but the present method used to identify the optimum level of expenditure seems extremely arbitrary. When asked to establish such a level the legislature may reply that half of the budgetary request would be reasonable. The university, on the other hand, may be equally nebulous and overly aggressive and optimistic in requesting funds.

The principles of VAMP can contribute substantially to the development of a proper level of progress and expenditure if it is coupled with predictions of economic growth, population growth, and the many other variables that come into play in preparing a long-range plan. But the maximum potential for VAMP is realized after the funding policy and restrictions have been established. On the basis of these decisions, VAMP principles and techniques can reveal the means to attain the most value for the monies allotted.

EXPANSION PROGRAM

Much of the university official's time is consumed in planning for expansion, and as each phase is completed new needs arise. The task is constant and extremely important. Expansion requires enormous expenditures, and the majority of costs are associated with building construction, land acquisition, equipment, and furniture. To insure that optimum value is achieved, value trade-offs should be developed early in the expansion program by relating the planned expenditure to the *type* of value the expenditure will represent.

The first major item that should be considered is land acquisition. If land is available in an acceptable area at a moderate market price or at no cost, and if expensive property with a view is also available for the building site, the difference in cost between the two proposals represents the *esteem value*. The estimated worth of the moderately priced or free land that is fully adequate for the university facilities is the *use value*. The relationship of use value and esteem value can be established in tabular form as shown in the following example:

Proposal	Cost	Use Value	Esteem Value
Adequate	$ 100,000	$100,000	$ 0
Bay view	500,000	100,000	400,000
Ocean view	1,000,000	100,000	900,000

Architectural designs for the building can also be evaluated on the basis of their use and esteem values. The architect can design an edifice that will rival the Taj Mahal in beauty, or he can create a building design that will accomplish the basic function without embellishment. Alternate designs should be considered, and the value relationships should be identified in the same manner as were the building site proposals.

Proposal	Cost	Use Value	Esteem Value
Adequate	$ 500,000	$500,000	$ 0
Modern	2,500,000	500,000	2,000,000
Gothic	4,000,000	500,000	3,500,000

The third major cost is for furniture and fixtures for the building; again, a wide range exists from the bare minimum to the most expensive.

Proposal	Cost	Use Value	Esteem Value
Adequate	$300,000	$300,000	$ 0
Fancy	600,000	300,000	300,000
Esthetic	900,000	300,000	600,000

Using the stated example and assuming that the cited costs are the only costs, a variety of combinations can be selected. At one extreme, a building could be erected for $900,000 including the purchase of the land that would fulfill the essential function of a university building. It would truly reflect use value and would represent the optimum to some factions of the populace. The completed building, however, would not be esthetically appealing.

A certain amount of esteem value is desirable in a university environment, but the degree of esteem value should be dependent upon the funds available for the program. If the funds were limited to $900,000 and building deferment was impractical, then the basic building that would adequately fulfill the requirements should be constructed. On the other hand, if unlimited funds were readily available, perhaps the $5 million complex consisting of $900,000 use value and $4.1 million esteem value would be entirely acceptable and proper. Under normal conditions (that is, budget limitations), these value trade-offs can be very helpful in arriving at the optimum program for a particular time under particular circumstances.

The partial use of VAMP could have obviated the furor when the officials of one university publicly lamented that a minor budget reduction of $90,000 was tantamount to university closure while they were buying extremely expensive view property for approximately $3 million in anticipation of future needs. Regardless of the esthetic aspects of the purchase, the use value represented by the $90,000 budget reduction so bitterly disputed should have been satisfied by the university officials *prior* to the expenditure of $3 million for a purchase with a relatively large future esteem value.

REDUCING EXISTING COSTS

Often a university is faced with an ever increasing number of students, increased faculty salaries, increased maintenance costs, and many other unpublicized costs without a commensurate increase in faculty or budget. This situation demands a reduction of existing costs and the reallocation of personnel capabilities, for which organization value analysis can be used to advantage. Instead of reverting to arbitrary budget decreases entailing corresponding student quota decreases, value priorities can be established. Tasks or activities that have marginal value can be eliminated while maintaining or increasing the effort devoted to the tasks and activities that have a high-value rating. An organization value analysis study can be initiated to increase the total value of the university while maintaining or decreasing the cost.

An OVAC could be developed to display the activities and tasks performed by the total faculty, and another OVAC could be created to depict the tasks and activities of the administrative services. For maximum advantage, both should be combined later on one chart representing the total activities and tasks of the university. The undertaking is formidable and will require many hours of effort. It is almost analogous to performing an industrial study encompassing an entire company.

The task of collecting the information needed to prepare a faculty OVAC would be monumental if the degree of participation normally requested during an industrial study were attempted. Fortunately, much of the required data are already available to the university officials. By using the university's class schedules and other existing documentation, making a few discreet telephone inquiries, and drawing on experience, an OVAC representing departmental averages can be developed with a fairly high degree of validity. The completed OVAC might resemble Exhibit 27.

Obviously, the example in the exhibit has been oversimplified and exaggerated to illustrate the organization value analysis approach. The analysis of the organization value analysis chart will establish the priority of activities. If the basic function is to instruct students, an inordinate amount of time is devoted to research. In the event of financial crisis the research time could be partially allocated to the other activities, thus relieving the immediate problem. Further analysis consisting of functional definitions and the development and evaluation of alternatives could increase the total value of the faculty organization by providing for innovations.

A similar OVAC should be developed for administrative services. Because of the lack of existing data and the diversity of the tasks performed, this study should be conducted in the same manner as those in industry. After both OVAC's have been analyzed and the proposed OVAC's have been developed, combining them can begin.

Exhibit 27

UNIVERSITY OVAC

CHARTED BY: Faculty Dean APPROVED BY: Dean

Act. No.	Activity (Verb-Noun)	Hrs. per Week	Cost per Week	% of Total	Engineering — Faculty (Typical) Tasks (Individual)	Hrs. per Week	Business — Faculty (Typical) Tasks (Individual)	Hrs. per Week	Anthropology — Faculty (Typical) Tasks (Individual)	Hrs. per Week	English — Faculty (Typical) Tasks (Individual)	Hrs. per Week	History — Faculty (Typical) Tasks (Individual)	Hrs. per Week
1	Prepare class	42		21.0	Draw up lesson plans	4	Draw up lesson plans	3			Draw up lesson plans	5	Draw up lesson plans	2
					Review papers	4	Review papers	7			Review papers	9	Review papers	8
2	Instruct students	52		26.0	Lecture	12	Lecture	8	Attend conference	6	Lecture	12	Lecture	12
							Moderate	2						
3	Counsel students	15		7.5	Advise	2	Advise	5	Analyze	3	Advise	2	Advise	3
4	Perform research	91		45.5	Attend lectures	4	Attend seminar	3	Go on field trips	15	Attend workshop	4	Attend lectures	5
					Do lab work	5	Do business reading	2	Write articles	6	Write book	8	Do history reading	5
					Do technical reading	2	Write book	10	Write book	10			Write book	5
					Write book	7								
	TOTAL	200		100		40		40		40		40		40

The combined university-level OVAC will require considerable effort on the part of the university officials, but the potential rewards will more than offset the inconveniences.

Aside from the direct benefits of reducing costs and increasing value, OVAC affords the university officials a complete financial-versus-activity overview which can be invaluable in obtaining support for budget increases. It translates the heretofore intangible university activities into definable, measurable outputs.

After analysis of the university-level OVAC and implementation of proposed cost-saving ideas, the quest for economies can progress to the area of procedures. Like industries, universities are guided by procedures, and a source of procedures for study is seldom lacking. The selection of a procedure for study depends upon the team formation.

Personnel within specific administrative functions can be formed into teams to study procedures germane to their functions. If a financially attractive procedure is identified that has universal application, the team could have one representative from each major function affected.

During a value analysis workshop at San Diego State College, three teams were established from the college's administrative staff. These teams, all representing the Division of Personnel Services, were instructed to select areas where difficulty had been experienced and, by using the techniques of value analysis, eliminate or reduce the problems.

The teams experienced some difficulty in selecting pertinent projects because their definitions of problem areas involved many abstractions. "How to increase the effectiveness of communication in the area" is typical of first attempts to state a problem for study. After some reflection on the difficulty of identifying the baseline of the existing effectiveness of communication, the teams resorted to projects of a tangible nature. One team selected the Placement Center annual report as a study project. The team prepared procedure flow charts, estimated the cost of developing the annual report, defined the functions, and developed alternatives. A different method of statistical sampling was proposed and implemented, and the report, which had been estimated to cost $22,000 annually, is now being compiled at an annual cost of $10,000. This saving of $12,000 was achieved with a total team effort of approximately 70 hours.

The other team results were impressive, although the savings achieved or the degree of value improvement accomplished was not as easily quantified. The significance of this study was the ease with which it was accomplished and the absence of apparent roadblocks. The team members were, for the most part, actively enthusiastic about the study and voiced intentions of continuing to use these techniques.

Another potential advantage of VAMP in education would be the inclusion of the VAMP philosophy and techniques in the university curriculum. Although it is a somewhat radical thought, training students who someday might enter business, government, or other fields susceptible to value improvement could avoid future costs.

The use of VAMP in education is not restricted to the university level. It can be applied to elementary schools, high schools, and junior colleges with equal effectiveness and in essentially the same manner. Perhaps even PTA's could avail themselves of the VAMP philosophy and adopt the functional approach.

The controversy concerning regional schools in some areas of the country could probably be resolved with the application of VAMP. A decision that schools should be situated within some arbitrary distance of all students has significantly increased costs. Instead of building one school to accommodate 3,000 students, five have to be constructed, each accommodating no more than 600 students. In addition to increased construction costs, this usually entails the removal of several acres of prime property from city tax rolls. The cost of five administrations and five cafeteria operations, for example, although not a linear increase from the cost of operating one facility, is also significant.

By using the functional approach to analysis, the cost of providing the essential function can be determined and evaluated. (The sociological aspects such as ethnic student mix, economic student mix, and specialized education would probably be considered secondary functions.) On the basis of the functional evaluation, the money in a relatively fixed budget could be spent in such a way as to obtain maximum value.

School bond issues often appear on the ballot. Their approval is generally advocated by teachers' associations, PTA's, school boards, and legislators. These people are convinced of the need for additional funds, but sometimes the voters are not, even though they may be sympathetic to education. They may believe that the funds requested do not represent true value. If a school district were to conduct an organization value analysis study for the district, relate the requested funds to specific functions, and publicize this information to the voters, the probability of bond issue passage would be greatly improved.

HOSPITALS

With the cost of medical care in hospitals soaring to new heights, there have been some claims that hospitals really do not cure ills; they merely transform them. A patient, physically ill and financially well on admittance, is discharged physically well and financially ill. The causes for these high costs are beyond the scope of this book. The simple fact that they exist is sufficient reason for VAMP application.

A U.S. Department of Labor report published in October 1968 examined medical cost increases over the previous 21 years and found that medical prices rose during the survey period 50 percent more than the cost of living did during the same period. Hospital room rates, for example, had increased by 354 percent during the period, while the cost of living, including medical costs, increased by 71 percent.

Hospitals deal with man's most valuable asset, his health. For health there are few cost-versus-function trade-offs that can be established. For this reason, hospital staff officials have not been known as aggressive cost-cutters. There have been attempts to reduce costs using normal cost-reduction techniques, but these attempts have often meant a decrease in some form of service. Several years ago hospitals began to hire business administrators in an effort to stem the meteoric rise in costs.

The commodity of a hospital differs so radically from an industrial commodity that many accepted business axioms have limited effect in this new environment. At what point is patient comfort, preparedness for emergency, research for new cures, and a thoroughly trained staff adequate? How can the value of these factors be quantified? Unhappily, even VAMP can't provide the solution to these problems, but it can be used to increase the value of the existing budget expenditures.

The previously mentioned Labor Department report also stated that wage costs account for approximately 65 percent of the total hospital operating costs, but higher wages contribute in only a minor way to the overall increase. The increase is primarily due to a vast expansion in the number of workers. Since the majority of costs are associated with employees, organization value analysis could have a significant effect in reducing costs or in avoiding future costs.

An OVAC of a hospital's nursing staff would probably result in many innovations that would increase the value of the nursing effort in patient care. Defining the basic and secondary functions would certainly be an interesting and worthwhile study, and the subsequent development of alternatives would introduce new methods. Similar OVAC's could be prepared for the medical staff to reduce the effort devoted to paperwork and increase the effort spent on medical activities. For example, alternative methods could be devised to fulfill the function of preparing insurance forms, surveys, special reports, and similar items. Of course, collecting data from physicians may require the use of sampling and estimating if data collection in the usual way proves impractical. However, physicians will definitely benefit from the study by the elimination of nonmedical chores from their routines, and this should provide the motivation for their full cooperation.

A combined OVAC—one that portrays the total activities and tasks of a hospital—could supply the incentives for many innovations in hospital administration including increased utilization of equipment and facilities. With medicare a reality, the need for additional hospital staffing and facilities could be reviewed in relation to the essential function of the hospital. This functional review would establish function-to-cost relationships useful in allocating existing funds and in planning for the future.

Another hospital area that can be served well by VAMP is that of procedures, both medical and business. Even though hospital *business* procedures have often come in for strong condemnation, the *medical* ones receive little criticism. Since the medical procedures, especially those of a control nature, deal with man's health, they are usually elaborate and totally uncompromising and allow for no deviation from the established standard. A minor discrepancy can result in a serious and costly incident.

Neither of these areas should be beyond the scope of analysis. Medical procedures can be subjected to procedure value analysis without fear of reducing safeguards because the safeguard features become part of the identified functions, and their continuance is guaranteed in the subsequent development of alternatives. The business procedures that should be analyzed are those that not only result in a substantial expenditure of money but also cause inconvenience to the patient or his family. In this way, two ends can be served by one means.

The hospital has long been viewed by the uninitiated as an institution of immense waste where daily charges exceed those of hotels on the French Riviera. The critics usually voice their comments, however, *after* they have been cured of some malady. While they were ailing, their health was beyond price; when they are cured, it is assigned a specific dollar value. (This assigned value will vary from 25 to 50 percent of the hospital bill.)

Some farsighted hospital administrators have already begun to introduce value engineering. One example is the Albert Einstein Medical Clinic in Philadelphia. Others have resorted to public relations specialists to combat adverse criticism. There is no better way to indicate to the public the sincere desire of the hospital staff to provide the patient with optimum care at minimum cost than to initiate an extensive VAMP program.

GOVERNMENT

Bureaucracies have seldom been accused of paperwork husbandry and organization frugality. Indeed, constant technological changes, sociological reforms, space explorations, and occasional wars dictate an ever increasing growth pattern for government. As the national production of goods and services increases, new uses are found for bureaucracies. But is this growth wasteful, or does it have value? The growth and cost are not per se undesirable.

The advice of many critics that government should operate with the same efficiency as private industry is theoretically logical but improbable in practice, for the individuals who occupy decision functions in government are somewhat handicapped. Their jobs lack permanence. If the executives in private industry were subject to possible replacement every two, four, or six years, the efficiency of private industry might not be exemplary. These periodic personnel adjustments can contribute significantly to the creation of redundant organizations and unnecessary procedures. Compounding this disadvantage is the opposite condition existing in the lower ranks of government. There civil service employees enjoy a job permanence that can be ended only by retirement. Another factor contributing to bureaucratic inefficiency is the great size of the governmental organization and the diversity of activities it performs.

The philosophy and techniques of VAMP are particularly useful in identifying and eradicating elements of poor or marginal value created by these conditions.

FEDERAL GOVERNMENT

The executives of the Federal Government are charged with many responsibilities, among which is the responsibility to spend money in large quantities. A good portion of this money is spent for salaries and represents a challenge for VAMP application. The methods and techniques used in applying VAMP to government are not appreciably different from those used in industry, and the roadblocks encountered may be fewer in number.

The Federal Government has aided the growth of value engineering from its formative years to the present by publicizing its benefits, advocating its use, and establishing extensive training programs. Indeed, the formation of value engineering organizations in many industries was stimulated by government suggestion. Evidence of government support for value engineering is found in the armed services procurement regulations. These stipulate that all contracts in excess of $100,000 must include a value engineering incentive clause that rewards the contractor for his value engineering achievements. Since the government was instrumental in promoting the use of value engineering, its acceptance of the VAMP philosophy and techniques may be equally enthusiastic.

The Federal Government has been in partnership with industry in the development and installation of many new management devices to control cost and improve efficiency. In fact, the first work distribution chart was a product of the Bureau of the Budget. Support for PERT, design work study, configuration control systems, and many other management techniques shown by the government, and especially by its military arm, indicates an objective, receptive mood.

The areas of opportunity in the executive branch of government do not differ greatly in concept from those of private industry. Federal organizations ordinarily conform to overall line and staff traditions; only the names are different. Almost every element of the Federal Government's executive organization can be duplicated in function by private industry. Therefore, the restrictions to VAMP application and the levels of plausible application are subject to the guidelines detailed earlier. For example, in a high-level analysis of federal agencies, OVAC could be very effective in highlighting possible redundancies among the agencies and in establishing a cost-to-function relationship of agency responsibilities. Entire governmental departments could be evaluated by organization value analysis; but, as in industry, the department director may not agree that such a study should be so all-encompassing. Conspiracy from within may be necessary.

The VAMP potential in government rests mainly in procedure value analysis, for government procedures have a far-reaching effect. They are binding on government employees and many of them spill over into private industry, causing the expenditure of millions of dollars. Procedure value analysis applied to government procedures can have an actual double-saving effect and a theoretical triple-saving effect. A reduction of cost achieved on a procedure affecting industry will save money for the government as well as for private industry. In addition, the increased industrial profits created by procedure cost reduction should increase the receipts of the Treasury Department, thus reducing the burden on the average taxpayer. Since the saving potential in such cases is at least double the usual potential, primary emphasis should be given to the external regulations, specifications, and requirements rather than to internal operating procedures.

An example of the potential in these areas is an estimate made by the National Federation of Independent Business which stated that some 342 million man-hours are spent each year by small businesses alone in filling out 200 federal and state questionnaires. This is equivalent to having more than 170,000 small business employees devote their entire yearly efforts to answering these questionnaires. The compiled data and subsequent reports, correlations, and projections, not to mention the cost of these manipulations, are of little use to the small businessman. His statistical requirements are modest.

Big business is also plagued with government requirements for information. The preparation of 2,000 different types of reports with some 250,000 copies yearly is not uncommon for large firms. Often the data required by government agencies are in such a format that new data-collection facilities must be set up to satisfy the requirements. This area of double-edged procedures clamors for analysis.

Even the judicial branch of the government may be able to avail itself of the philosophy and techniques of VAMP. With court calendars lengthening, perhaps some new trial procedures may be more efficient than adding judges, building new courthouses, and backlogging court cases. Both procedure value analysis and organization value analysis could be used to develop other ways to accomplish the functions.

The judicial branch of the Federal Government and the entire legal profession would probably benefit immensely if the functional approach were applied to courtroom procedures and legal jargon. The tradition involved is recognized as sacred, but whereas industry and science have progressed out of necessity and in spite of roadblocks, the legal profession holds firm to the old order. Traditions may have esteem value and may guard an old profession, but existing practices based solely on tradition are particularly susceptible to the functional approach to value.

State Government

State governments are not totally unlike the Federal Government and have many common areas of VAMP potential. They are directed by elected or appointed officials and contain the same inhibitions to efficiency as does the Federal Government. Although the diversity of activities is not proportionally less, a state government is theoretically less cumbersome to the total application of VAMP than is the Federal Government. The double-saving benefits that apply in the Federal Government—that is, the saving to the businessman as well as to the state—are present and represent an attractive potential for cost reduction and maximum value. Yet few state governments have applied the functional approach to their operations.

The few states that have installed or are contemplating the installation of a value analysis program—Massachusetts, Pennsylvania, California, Michigan, Illinois, Ohio, and Iowa—have been impressed with its potential. For example, Pennsylvania identified potential savings in excess of $3 million in one value analysis seminar. The governor of Massachusetts determined that the benefits of value analysis were so important that he established the "Executive Council for Value Analysis."

Value analysis programs in state government have already saved millions of dollars on the hardware type of projects, but they cannot cope with organization or procedure expenditures; for these VAMP is needed. The introduction of VAMP to state government operations need not be a complex maneuver. A governor, when apprised of the potential benefits to the state, to businessmen, and to himself, cannot logically refuse it admittance.

The problem is to inform the governor. The average governor, contrary to the belief of some voters, cannot spend many hours at the country club and maintain an efficient government. His responsibilities and duties are many, and the investigation of every new cost-reduction technique would probably occupy most of his time, leaving none for administration. The VAMP potential should be presented to the chief executive of a state in much the same way that it is presented to the chief executive of a company. The presentation must contain evidence of past success and expectation of future success sufficient to stimulate the governor to action. Unlike industry, where the indifference of the chief executive is sufficient for the introduction of VAMP, the peculiarities of governmental operations require the active support and enthusiasm of the leader to attain any degree of success.

CITY GOVERNMENT

The government of the average large city probably has more opportunities to use VAMP than has the state or the Federal Government. The operation of a city, whether by a mayor, a city council, a city manager, or some combination of these, is closer to the voter. As a result, the voter can trace any large expenditure directly to his pocket, and he reacts at the polls to wasteful or uneconomic operations.

In addition, the average citizen is much better informed concerning the total operation of the city government. Individually he feels that he is more of a force in changing or retaining the city management because one voice in a city of 100,000 voices can be heard much more distinctly than can one voice in a state of 3 million or a nation of 200 million voices. Therefore, the political aspects and advantages offered by VAMP should be sufficient reasons in themselves for enthusiastic adoption by the municipal authorities.

A multitude of services performed by the city government, because of their repetitive nature and extensive use, are normally more conducive to analysis by VAMP techniques than are state government activities. The data-collection task is also made easier by the geographical boundaries of the city. The political pressure on city officials to maintain the operating budget at the same level year after year or to increase it at a rate well below economic trends is constant. At the same time, there is voter demand to maintain or increase services while decreasing the cost to the taxpayers.

It is not uncommon, for example, to have the voters reject passage of police bonds in the solitude of the voting booth while advocating vociferously the need for increased police protection and better crime fighting equipment the same evening. Fire departments are often faced with the same paradox.

When increased services are demanded and the budget expenditure level must remain constant, an organization value analysis study can be put to work to satisfy both requirements. The development of alternative methods to accomplish the essential functions of the police department, fire department, trash collections, or any other sizable service would undoubtedly uncover ingenious and probably unorthodox ways to satisfy the essential function more fully with no increase in cost.

In addition to the cost-reduction potential, OVAC wall charts can be invaluable in improving personnel morale, in planning for future expansion, and in requesting additional funds. Yet few city governments are even mildly interested in investigating the benefits offered by the functional approach. With the exception of Baltimore and Chicago, attempts to install value engineering programs in city governments throughout the country have met with little response. In one large Western city, the local chapter of the Society of American Value Engineers offered the services of several of its members to assist in setting up a value engineering program at no cost to the city. The letter containing this offer was never even acknowledged.

Yet city governments will contract with a management consultant who will identify areas of potential improvement, explain what measures should be taken, and leave. For true economy, the city officials themselves must be trained to identify areas of opportunity and must be equipped with the techniques required to exploit those opportunities. It is to be hoped that in the future VAMP principles and techniques will be investigated and evaluated at the city level.

* * *

The use of VAMP in schools, hospitals, and government is not revolutionary. In fact, these areas have been given special attention in relation to VAMP only because they have long been considered beyond the realm of normal business practices. Actually, the only prerequisite for the use of VAMP is the existence of an organization or a procedure regardless of whether it is in private industry or in the public sector.

12

Designing a VAMP Program

THE key to success in the design and installation of a VAMP program is planning. The depth and care exercised during the planning phase will determine the degree of program success as well as the quantity and intensity of future roadblocks to implementation. The planning elements that are inherent in any program plan must be considered with an eye to such company characteristics as the type of leadership exercised, the type of organization, the corporate objectives, and other features that differentiate one company from another. Each VAMP program must be tailored to fit a particular company.

The planning considerations for the design and implementation of a VAMP program in this chapter are directed primarily toward the profit-oriented industrial company, but they can be applied to any type of organization with minor variations in the approach.

PROGRAM PURPOSE

The purpose of a VAMP program could be masked in a variety of high-flown terms, but a simple explanation is the quest for profit improvement. This reason by itself does not set VAMP apart from any other management endeavor, for all elements of business should contribute directly or indirectly to the profit development of a company. Profit can be increased without the use of VAMP. For example, the selling price of the product can be increased, resulting—theoretically—in a proportional enlargement of profits. Or profit can be extended by an increase in sales volume. But these methods have disadvantages which preclude their general use. Competition, market demands, and government regulations often render these theoretical adjustments impractical, ineffectual, or illegal.

The easiest way to increase profit is to reduce operating costs. This can be done at any time, and it has an immediate impact on the profit and loss statement. In addition, it can result in a more desirable competitive position. In the average company there are many forces at work to accomplish this. Typical cost reduction programs include value engineering, employee suggestion, and management improvement subprograms. Industrial engineering techniques, created to attain optimum efficiency, are also widely employed to reduce costs. But these current cost-reduction efforts are for the most part directed at and restricted to hardware applications. Although the cost of paperwork and organization has long been recognized as a significant contributor to total operating cost, little has been done to attack these costs in a logical and meaningful manner. VAMP was designed *specifically* to close this loophole.

A secondary purpose of a VAMP program is to improve employee morale. The employees who participate in or are subjects of a VAMP study become motivated to greater efficiency. An experiment conducted more than 40 years ago at the Western Electric Company revealed that increased light in a specific work area could increase the productivity of the employees in that area. Conversely, a decrease of the work-area lighting would also increase employee productivity. The experimenters concluded that the degree of illumination was immaterial; this new efficiency was simply a result of employee recognition. The same effect is noticed during a VAMP study when the employees can identify with company objectives.

In VAMP studies where there is no threat of employee termination, morale improvement is appreciably greater than it is in a study undertaken to reduce employment. The unthreatening instance represents to the employee an attempt by the company to improve some aspect of his job. Since he will benefit from the study, his personal involvement will be assured and his morale will improve.

The use of VAMP also promotes improved managerial communication. The team action of VAMP plus the many and varied conversations required during the study information phase fosters better working relationships among managers. In addition, managers who participate in a VAMP study develop a better understanding of and increased respect for their fellow managers' functions. This can aid in molding and strengthening the entire management unit by increasing managerial skills in communicating with others.

OBJECTIVES

The broad objectives of a VAMP program would be primarily the satisfaction of the program purposes previously delineated. Since these purposes are difficult to measure, the methods used to attain the purposes become the program objectives. A typical list of these objectives may include the following.

1. *Establishing VAMP specialists and generalists.* At first thought, it may seem that a company of VAMP specialists would be more desirable than a mixture of specialists and generalists, and this misconception has hastened the demise of some new management techniques. If the company managers have sufficient time available to become VAMP specialists, there is some probability that all business activity will cease prior to the completion of the first VAMP training seminar. Managers do have other concerns. The objective is to train managers so that they can *participate* in VAMP studies under the guidance of a specialist. A basic knowledge of the techniques and principles is sufficient for the generalists. How many specialists and generalists should be trained depends upon the size and nature of the company and the potential for VAMP exploitation.

2. *Attaining companywide recognition of VAMP.* This objective should be planned early in the program to ease the introduction of VAMP. Orientation presentations, articles in the company newspaper, and other forms of public relations can lower many barriers to the acceptance of VAMP. If the study subjects have prior knowledge of the purposes of VAMP, the fear and skepticism sometimes encountered is reduced. Also, the publicity adds authority and implies com-

pany endorsement which is invaluable in securing the appointment of subjects for VAMP studies.

3. *Establishing study selection criteria.* An important objective of the program is to provide means and methods of selecting the most suitable projects for VAMP studies. The arbitrary selection of projects will not increase the likelihood of success. The potential projects must be strategically evaluated, especially during the early phases of the program.

4. *Establishing and directing training programs.* A VAMP training program should be designed to provide trained personnel sufficient to perform studies at each level of organization. The training should be assigned to the educational or training department in companies where such departments have been established, but the type and frequency of training, the selection of students, and the selection of the projects should be left to the director of the VAMP program.

5. *Providing a consulting service.* The organization and establishment of a small staff of VAMP specialists to perform as consultants is recommended. When the principles and techniques of VAMP have been accepted throughout the company, several managers may wish to conduct studies in their areas. Without some group that can provide consulting services to these managers, the potential saving represented by their requests will be lost.

PROGRAM SCHEDULE

An effective program plan must contain planning milestones against which progress toward accomplishing the objectives can be measured. To do this, a time schedule must be set up. Each basic objective should be assigned an estimated completion date, and each identifiable action that must be taken to accomplish the stated objective should be scheduled in a similar manner. If the measurement of progress toward an objective is difficult or impractical, the steps in attaining the objectives can be scheduled. For example, the objective of establishing and directing a training program contains recurring and nonrecurring actions. This objective can be expressed in a program plan as shown in Exhibit 28. When all the specified actions have been completed, the target is considered to have been reached.

The detailed schedule is a significant part of the plan to establish a

Exhibit 28

PROGRAM PLAN

	JANUARY 2 9 16 23 30	FEBRUARY 6 13 20 27	MARCH 6 13 20 27	APRIL 3 10 17 24	MAY 1 8 15 22 29	JUNE 5 12 19 26
DETERMINE TYPE OF TRAINING	▶					
DETERMINE QUANTITY TO BE TRAINED	▶					
DETERMINE CURRICULUM		▶				
ESTABLISH TRAINING SCHEDULE		▶				
SCHEDULE PROJECT SELECTION			▶			
SCHEDULE STUDENT SELECTION				▶		
SCHEDULE SPEAKER SELECTION				▶		
COORDINATE REQUIREMENTS WITH TRAINING DEPARTMENT				▶		
FOLLOW UP TRAINING DEPARTMENT ACTION					▶	▶

VAMP program, but the introductory timing should also be considered in order to increase the potential for success. Should the introduction of a VAMP program be delayed if a major reorganization is anticipated? Should it be applied to existing organizations or to new ones? Is the management attitude conducive to acceptance, or should attempts to revise attitudes be scheduled first? The approach is vitally important, and the answers to these questions, which will depend on the company's environment, should be carefully weighed prior to implementation.

PROGRAM ADMINISTRATION

What organization should administer the VAMP program? This will depend partly on the organizational structure of the company and partly on the attitude of company officials. VAMP's nature does not limit its administration to any one specialized area, and many areas of a typical company are well suited to conduct VAMP operations. However, placing this function on a staff level reporting directly to the company president has many obvious advantages; the most important of these is obtaining the support of the president.

In the evaluation of major departments, the maximum value potential of VAMP is at the president's staff level. If, for example, the controller's function conducted an objective and valid organization value analysis study of the engineering department, the proposed improvements might be roadblocked by the engineering manager for obvious reasons. Since the organizational status of the engineering manager and the controller is usually similar, the result may well be a standoff.

The arguments for establishing a VAMP program at the presidential staff level are substantial; but almost the same arguments can be proposed for value engineering, work simplification, or any other discipline that crosses normal organizational lines. If the president were to assume command of all these disciplines, his ability to function as a chief executive would be hampered so seriously that the company, despite its streamlined management team, would be on the road to bankruptcy. The establishment of a VAMP program may therefore be relegated to a lower level of organization. As success is experienced at the lower levels, attempts can be made to upgrade the level of reporting. Until that time several other prime areas can be considered.

VAMP in Industrial Engineering

In those companies that are fortunate enough to have a strong industrial engineering department, VAMP may find a reasonable home there. Industrial engineering crosses organizational lines of responsibility, is aware of potential projects, and is cost-oriented. In addition, the industrial engineering organization often reports to the company's chief executive, which is a further reason for placing VAMP there.

However, assigning VAMP to the industrial engineering department may have drawbacks. Since VAMP is a mixed discipline that contains inherent criticism of some work simplification techniques, its new parents may hinder its effectiveness and withhold the emphasis needed to promote VAMP successfully. On the other hand, if the attitudes of the manager and his staff are favorable toward VAMP principles and techniques, its advancement and application could prosper.

VAMP in Value Engineering

The value engineering department would also seem to be a reasonable choice for administering a VAMP program because the analytical techniques are taken from value engineering. Value engineers are already imbued with the functional approach idea, and the introduction of work simplification techniques should be accepted without inordinate resistance. The purist may object, but fortunately the purist is vanishing from value engineering. The value engineering department would therefore be an excellent foster organization for VAMP if the department itself has attained company acceptance. Unfortunately, value engineering in many companies is suspect because of its newness, and in many others it has not been used at all.

In those companies where value engineering is not practiced diligently and openly and where it has not reached the degree of company acceptance enjoyed by other service organizations, the inclusion of a VAMP program is not recommended. The addition of a new discipline to one not firmly entrenched may endanger both.

There is another possible reason for not automatically placing VAMP in the value engineering department. Value engineering has not yet achieved the organizational stability and stature of other long-established service disciplines. In some companies the value engineering efforts are restricted to the engineering departments; in other companies to the purchasing department; and in still others to the controller's department. Some value engineering departments are staff; others are line. This lack of uniformity requires that each company assess its value engineering organization to determine the suitability and probability of VAMP program success in its value engineering environment.

VAMP IN COST REDUCTION

As the use of cost-plus-fixed-fee contracts has waned and as competition has become acute, price has again gained predominance and cost-reduction programs have sprung up across the land. In the wake of this popularity, books were published, consulting firms were established, and training seminars were developed to further the art and science of cost reduction. To demonstrate responsiveness to government cost-reduction campaigns, many companies established formal cost-reduction programs. Those established for the primary purpose of profit improvement rather than for publicity purposes offer an excellent and logical staging area for VAMP if—

1. Cost reduction has been accepted and is practiced seriously.
2. The cost-reduction organization is stable and efficient.
3. The full-time cost-reduction manager reports at a level of organization high enough to promise successful VAMP implementation.
4. The cost-reduction organization contains such elements or categories of cost reduction as employee suggestions, value engineering, and methods improvement.

One disadvantage of including VAMP in a formal cost-reduction program is the connotation that has been assigned to the words "cost reduction." To many, cost reduction, efficiency experts, time study, and the rest mean only one thing—termination of employees. These individuals will develop ingenious barriers against fruitful implementation of VAMP. If this connotation is prevalent in a particular company, other areas should be examined for a better environment.

The newness of cost-reduction programs has spawned myriad organizational formations which, like value engineering organizations, must be considered individually before a final determination can be made. This diversity precludes a universal endorsement of cost-reduction programs as the most suitable to administer a VAMP program.

VAMP in Systems and Procedures

Usually a large or moderately large company will have a specific organization that is responsible for developing, coordinating, and publishing corporate procedures. The organization may be called management systems, systems and procedures, or program planning, among others, depending upon the type, size, and nature of the company. This organization warrants particular attention in determining the best administrative location for a VAMP program for the following reasons:

1. The employees of these organizations—the analysts—are well versed in charting techniques and often have an extensive background in work simplification. To train the analysts in VAMP would require only the addition of selected value engineering techniques, thereby decreasing the training period significantly.
2. This organization is the source of many procedures, and the introduction of VAMP techniques to procedure development can help appreciably to curtail costs.
3. The analysts are aware of complex and expensive procedures and can provide an abundant supply of study projects.
4. A systems and procedures group is usually an accepted and respected organization which has developed rapport with all the other company departments.
5. The employees are usually viewed as experts in devising paperwork systems and are often asked to help in resolving difficult procedural problems. This type of consulting operation is helpful in expanding the VAMP effort.

6. By its very nature a systems and procedures organization has free access to all other organizations, and this overview can provide many lucrative projects for organization value analysis.
7. In many companies, the systems and procedures organization controls or is associated with the computer facility, where many economies can be achieved.

If the systems and procedures group reports to a reasonably high level of management, and if it can be transformed from a systems-oriented to a function-oriented organization without too much difficulty, it should rate high on the list of potential administrators.

STAFFING A VAMP ORGANIZATION

Each VAMP organization must be tailored to the needs of a particular company. Unhappily, there are no known mathematical formulas that can be applied to the many variables in order to arrive at the optimum in staffing. The potential value improvement and the staff or line relationships with other organizations affect this decision. For example, if VAMP principles and techniques were taught to the existing systems and procedures analysts, additional personnel might not be required to perform procedure value analysis. The analysts would do this as part of their regular assignment. However, they may not be in a position to expand the use of organization value analysis. Some other group would then have to perform this function, which may not represent the best in VAMP organization.

The most analytical method to determine personnel staffing requirements is to use OVAC. By building an organization with organization value analysis, adjusted to fit the company's peculiar variables, the optimum in VAMP organization should be achieved. There are some aspects of a VAMP organization that are common, and broad guidelines can be developed to increase the probability of success.

VAMP DIRECTOR

If a VAMP program is to be effective, someone must be assigned the responsibility of directing it. This must be a full-time assignment.

A task of this nature is often put in the hands of a staff employee as a corollary function, to be performed when and if he has the time. Seldom is this approach acceptable, for the effort that must be expended to initiate a VAMP program demands full-time attention. Unaided, VAMP cannot create its own acceptance. The qualities that the VAMP leader should possess are a demonstrated ability to get a job done and managerial abilities that are widely respected throughout the company. The task should be given to a dynamic innovator. Success or failure depends primarily on the abilities of the program director.

Whether to fill the position with an existing company manager or search outside the company for an appropriate candidate deserves consideration. The company manager is usually aware of company eccentricities, has developed rapport with other managers, is knowledgeable about all operations, and has proved himself competent. However, this close and long association with the company may have generated some self-imposed roadblocks detrimental to the exploitation of VAMP potential. He may "know" that VAMP *cannot* succeed within certain areas. A recently hired manager has no such knowledge and may succeed precisely because he doesn't know that it can't be done. Also, there is an air of uncertainty that surrounds a newly hired manager, especially if he is said to be an authority. This can be advantageous. Since the new manager's actions cannot be predicted from past experience, the cooperation he receives may exceed that offered to the man whose reactions *are* predictable. In addition, the new manager may be better able to identify areas of high cost and low value because of his lack of ingrained bias.

The selection factors involved in evaluating possible candidates to establish and maintain an excellent VAMP program should be given considerable thought by upper-level management. Although the perfect candidate—one who possesses all the attributes of the good manager—is a hypothetical composite, the criteria of productivity and professional proficiency can insure an acceptable selection.

VAMP STAFF

As a rule the VAMP director will require a staff. The functions of the staff will vary with the program plan, but, if OVAC is used to develop the VAMP organization, the activities and tasks will be clearly identified. Once the size of the staff is determined, the selection of individuals becomes paramount. The VAMP director should use care in choosing his staff members, for future company opinion of the VAMP program will be based on their attitudes and actions and they will be largely responsible for the subsequent success or failure of the program.

The criteria used to choose the director can also be applied to the staff. The ability to do a job and a facility for developing rapport are the most important qualities of a candidate. A strong analytic mind is also important. The staff should include people of diverse experience and backgrounds and of different age groupings. Coupling the older, experienced company employee with the young, inexperienced but dynamic employee can produce a synergistic effect.

TRAINING

To be effective, the director and his staff must be thoroughly trained in the use of VAMP techniques, and this training cannot be gleaned from books alone. Practical application under controlled conditions is a prerequisite to guiding others in VAMP studies. The ability to select suitable projects, form study teams, and guide team efforts increases with continued application. The necessary training can be acquired in workshop seminars, as explained in Chapter 10, but in the initial phase of setting up a program trained instructors may be lacking. To fill this temporary void, the use of a consultant or attendance at an industrywide workshop seminar is recommended. If a consultant is retained, the VAMP director should assure himself that the selected consultant's knowledge of VAMP is sufficient to warrant the expenditure.

METHODS OF IMPLEMENTATION

An edict by the company president to establish and conduct a VAMP program is probably the most effective method of VAMP introduction. Many mundane problems regarding funding, responsibility, and organizational stature are resolved instantly. For reasons discussed earlier, however, the president may not exhibit such a high degree of confidence in VAMP until he can evaluate the results. Where this occurs, the problems reappear and decisions must be made.

Should the VAMP program be initiated on a companywide basis with publicity and promises, or should a nucleus be established with a planned gradual expansion? The former has the advantage of informing many people at one time and quickening widespread acceptance and cooperation. It also has the danger of failing. If the introduction is enthusiastic but well-trained personnel are lacking, the results of the first study may be marginal and may discredit the original claims. The method of VAMP introduction, in which experience and training are gained prior to a formal debut, is the more cautious of the two. But this method, too, has its perils. During the time when the VAMP effort is being kept small and inconspicuous, the company can be losing thousands of dollars in potential savings. Moreover, an initially small VAMP effort is in danger of being strangled by a larger and more influential foe. The important factor in the decision is the degree of proficiency exhibited by the VAMP director.

PROGRAM FUNDING

Normally the question of funding the VAMP effort will be raised at program onset and at least semiannually thereafter. The skeptics will insure this review. Also, since a program of this nature is usually determined to be an indirect rather than a direct charge cost, any request for funding will be subject to additional scrutiny.

In some industries indirect charge costs are treated as the only type of real expense; those costs that are direct charges are regarded as a kind of *quasi*-expense and seldom questioned. In the wake of this philosophy, there are constant attempts to change a normally indirect charge to a direct charge and thereby achieve cost reductions. Regardless of the misconceptions involved, the tendency to challenge all indirect potential costs is always present.

There are several ways to fund a VAMP effort. Many of these were developed to accommodate value engineering programs, which also have encountered similar funding problems. One method is to establish a VAMP budget bank. Under this system, the required funding is borrowed from this bank and the loan is repaid from a predetermined percentage of the savings achieved as a result of VAMP studies. If the savings accruing to the VAMP organization exceed the total cost of the VAMP effort, then this effort can be expanded to consume the excess or the predetermined percentage share can be reduced.

Another method requires that the organization benefiting from the VAMP effort reimburse the VAMP organization from the savings achieved in the study. Both of these methods are really no more than bookkeeping games which may hinder rather than aid the VAMP effort. The first method may subjectively promote the inflation of claimed savings so as to expand the effort and return the loaned budget quickly. The second method, requiring the benefiting department to transfer budget to the VAMP organization, will undoubtedly entail haggling. The benefiting organization will estimate the VAMP saving extremely conservatively, since a portion of the saving will be removed from its own operating budget. The more the budget is exceeded, the more conservative the estimate will become. The VAMP organization, on the other hand, will develop a more generous estimate of the saving for obvious reasons. As a result, a spirit of antagonism can replace one of cooperation.

The most effective and logical way to fund the VAMP effort is to create a budget based on the program objectives and the tasks that are specified on OVAC. VAMP should be recognized as a normal overhead cost similar to other service organizations, and unnecessary or marginal bookkeeping systems for the sole purpose of justifying the VAMP expense should be avoided. If the program is conducted properly, the justification will become evident without the use of detailed ledgers and journals. However, it is true that in some companies these games are necessary to overcome initial resistance. In these instances, their use should be discontinued as soon as VAMP acceptance has been gained.

Savings Validation

If the effectiveness of VAMP is to be measured by dollar savings, or if the results are to be included in a cost-reduction program report of some sort, the saving claims must be valid. Cost-reduction claims can evoke cynical disbelief because of the bad reputation attached to some cost-reduction programs. To keep this stigma away from the VAMP program, only those results should be claimed that can be documented and validated by audit. For example, if a procedural value analysis study results in a reduction of procedure elements representing 2,000 man-hours per year, the reduction is normally reported as a cost saving. However, the VAMP organization should *not* claim the reduction as a saving until the disposition of the hours saved has been determined. If, as a result of the study, the employees have 2,000 hours of additional coffee breaks, there is no net increase in value. But, if the staff has been reduced or new tasks of value are being performed, the saving can be considered valid.

Study results that achieve a reduction of man-hours less than the equivalent of one man-year or that are spread over many organizations, each of which benefits in a small way, are difficult to identify; and the profitable disposition of these hours usually must be assumed. When man-hour savings are substantial, however, their disposition must be ascertained prior to any public claims of success. The skeptics wait to disprove one heralded example and thereby destroy the confidence in VAMP that has been established. As a further precaution, it is recommended that any achieved saving of significant magnitude be subjected to an audit by an internal audit organization or a parallel function. Such an audit will increase credibility and discourage skeptics.

*   *   *

There is no stereotyped VAMP program that can be inserted mechanically in the universal business computer to produce results. Every program must be tailored to fit the individual needs, potential, and conditions of a particular company or agency. The purpose of the program and the planning objectives required to fulfill the purpose should be itemized in detail, and the estimated accomplishment of each should be scheduled. An examination of the existing organizational structure is necessary to determine the areas best suited to the administration of the proposed VAMP program, for VAMP is per se a business orphan. The lack of natural business parents creates a variety of possible and plausible organization adopters, each of which should be evaluated. The one that offers the greatest likelihood of future VAMP growth is the logical choice.

The selection and training of the VAMP director and his staff is of considerable importance, since these individuals will develop and project the VAMP image throughout the company. The VAMP background and training of these employees will determine the relative ease of program implementation. The number of employees required to accomplish the program objectives can be best determined by using OVAC.

Although the investigation and evaluation of each planning element is important, the selection of the individual to lead the VAMP effort deserves the most careful consideration. An excellent director can offset many planning deficiencies, whereas even the best plan cannot compensate for an ineffective leader.

Appendix

VAMP Workshop
Seminar Curriculum

T<small>HE</small> following is a typical curriculum for a 40-hour VAMP workshop seminar conducted on 10 successive workdays. The sessions are 4 hours long with 15 minutes of each session allocated to a coffee break.

FIRST SESSION

1. *Introduction to VAMP Seminar—Guest Speaker (30 minutes)*. During the introduction the guest speaker should emphasize the following:

    a. The present estimated cost of paperwork.
    b. The interdependence of paperwork and organization.
    c. The past attempts to solve the paperwork problem.
    d. The need for a new management discipline.
    e. The immediate training objectives.
    f. The company's long-range training objectives.

g. The reasons why these particular managerial students were selected as participants.

h. What is expected from the participants.

2. *The Functional Approach—Guest Speaker (90 minutes).* This period of instruction is the most critical of the training, for without a complete understanding of the functional approach all subsequent efforts will be wasted. The lesson objective is to provide the student with sufficient training to enable him to—

a. Determine the functions of procedures and organizations by using the two-word functional definition.

b. Classify the functions as either basic or secondary.

c. Develop a value rating for the functions defined.

The teaching of the functional approach is facilitated by the use of hardware examples. The students can grasp the physical characteristics of the hardware and learn to identify and categorize its functions much more easily than they can the functions of procedures or organizations. After the students understand and have practiced the functional approach using the hardware examples, they can apply the techniques to procedures and organizations.

3. *Organization Value Analysis Chart—Instructors (105 minutes).* OVAC has to be introduced early in the seminar to allow sufficient time for the projects. The employees of the organizations being studied must collect and record data for three days, during which time the seminar instructor can continue in procedure value analysis. Although such a brief survey is not the optimum in organization value analysis, an extension of this period would entail lengthening the seminar. The objectives of this lesson are to teach the student—

a. The evolution of OVAC from the work simplification chart.

b. The overall procedure used to conduct a study.

c. The detailed methods of preparing the OVAC preliminary forms: the task data sheet, the task list, and the activity list.

d. The preparation of OVAC.

A generous supply of examples and visual aids should be used during this lesson to insure a firm understanding of the philosophy and techniques. Considerable emphasis should be placed on distinguishing between an activity and a task. The differences are often somewhat nebulous and difficult to explain, but to confuse one with the other can invalidate the entire study. Student participation in these drills is recommended.

SECOND SESSION

1. *OVAC; Class Application—Instructor* (*105 minutes*). This period of instruction gives the students the opportunity to practice preparing the OVAC supporting forms and OVAC itself, using canned examples. During this time the techniques are reviewed and each team prepares one chart on the basis of information supplied by the instructor. The same examples are used for all teams.

Only the information phase of the job plan is covered in this lesson, since the remaining phases are based on the completed OVAC. It is the responsibility of the project leaders to insure that the information phase is covered adequately and that the teams do not focus on insignificant details. Because the time allowed for this session is minimal, each minute must be used productively.

2. *OVAC; Project Work—Instructor* (*120 minutes*). With some basic instruction from the teaching staff, the teams begin the OVAC information phase of their selected projects. This entails introducing the subjects of the study—the organizations—to the data-collection process. The teams provide sufficient forms for the study, instruct the study subjects on preparing the forms, establish a schedule for completion, and answer questions. The best way to accomplish this is to assemble the employees of the chosen organizations in a conference room or a classroom to hear an explanation of the role they play in the VAMP seminar. An excellent training aid in presenting this material is a 20-minute film entitled *The Work Distribution Chart* which is available from the Union Bank of California. Although this film does not satisfy the analysis requirements of organization value analysis, it covers the preparation of the work distribution chart (which is akin to the preparation of OVAC) in an adequate and entertaining way.

THIRD SESSION

1. *The Procedure Flow Chart—Instructor* (*45 minutes*). The purpose of this lesson is to acquaint the students with the procedure flow chart. The instructor begins the session by discussing (a) the reasons for using the procedure flow chart, (b) the types of charts, (c) the desired depth of charting, (d) the corollary benefits of procedure flow charting, and (e) the techniques of collecting the necessary data. The procedure flow chart is introduced at this time because no further team action can be

devoted to OVAC until the employees of the project organizations complete the OVAC data-collection phase.

Collecting the data required for the procedure projects must be inaugurated early in the seminar to insure project completion. As with the introduction of OVAC, an ample quantity of examples is recommended. Since the level of detail is very important in constructing a procedure flow chart, the simple warning to use only essential detail is inadequate and examples are needed to establish some standards.

2. *Procedure Flow Chart; Class Application—Instructor (90 minutes).* During this period the class participates by preparing procedure flow charts. Each team is given a written description of a procedure in chronological order. The teams reduce the description to a listing of discrete elements and then transfer the listing to a wall-size symbolic representation. The project leaders should guide the teams and assist when necessary. Upon completion of the wall charts, each captain presents his team's answer to the procedure example in a brief discourse. The instructor should stimulate and direct student discussion, always keeping in mind the tight time schedule. After each team presents its project, the instructor conducts his critique. He identifies to the class members the areas in which their charting conforms to the theory, and he pinpoints the areas where it does not. This critique also helps the students to determine the proper level of detail. Since all the teams chart the same procedure, the instructor can make comparisons.

3. *Procedure Flow Chart; Project Work—Instructor (90 minutes).* Equipped with the theory and some practice, the teams begin their project work to prepare a procedure flow chart that depicts the procedure that is under consideration. At this time, the captain should assign to each team member a specific area of the procedure for which he will be responsible. By allocating these areas, the task of data collection is reduced and expedited. Since the data must be collected by actual observation, the team members move to their areas of assignment. The meeting room should be made available to the students during the entire project work period and for the remainder of the day. The teams that want to spend additional nonseminar time on their projects should not be discouraged from doing so.

FOURTH SESSION

1. *Procedure Flow Chart; Project Work—Instructor (120 minutes).* Although this period is a continuation of the previous day's effort in project work, the teams should gather in the meeting room at the appointed

time. This assures continued team membership and allows the captains an opportunity to tell of any particular roadblocks encountered thus far in the information phase. Also, it gives the teams a chance to consolidate the data already collected. After this brief meeting the teams continue the information phase for the remainder of the period.

2. *Human relations; Habits and Attitudes—Guest Speaker (105 minutes).* This lesson is intended to prepare the student for the inevitable roadblocks he will encounter in the pursuit of VAMP projects or any proposals involving change. The identification of these roadblocks will not constitute new learning for the student, since he has probably read many articles on the subject. However, by discussing the habits and attitudes that help create roadblocks, the student will develop a keener awareness of or sensitivity to the importance of human relations. Understanding the human relations aspects will better equip him to identify potential roadblocks and to plan for their avoidance. *The Engineering of Agreement*, a training film available from Roundtable Productions, 275 South Street, Beverly Hills, California, is particularly valuable in emphasizing the principles and techniques of human relations. It is shown during this period.

FIFTH SESSION

1. *Procedure Value Analysis; Project Work—Instructor (120 minutes).* In this session the teams continue to collect data for their assigned procedure projects. As in previous project work sessions, before dispersing to gather data the teams meet to discuss any major problems encountered thus far. This period should conclude the search for data.

2. *Procedure Flow Chart Preparation—Instructor (105 minutes).* The collected data are compiled by each team and the wall-size procedure flow chart is constructed during this session. At this point the project leaders become very important; it is their job to guide the teams during the preparation of the wall charts. If the teams' early efforts are reflected in an unnecessarily detailed and complex chart, the project leaders should suggest ways to improve the presentation. During this period the instructor should point out any radical departures from the guidelines.

SIXTH SESSION

1. *OVAC Preparation—Instructor (120 minutes).* By the sixth session the completed OVAC preliminary forms have been collected from the project organization. Now the teams attempt to understand the collected

data. They review the task data sheets and prepare the task lists, reserving judgment on the interpretation of the data and the objectivity of the employees collecting and recording the information. The instructor should emphasize that the time restrictions of the seminar can account for many inaccuracies and that, in the operational mode, organization value analysis studies would afford the subjects more instruction and more time to complete the forms.

After the task lists are prepared, the original activity list is adjusted accordingly. From this amalgamated information the wall chart is prepared. The instructor and the project leaders assist the teams by providing guidance as required.

2. *OVAC and Procedure Flow Charts Presentation* (*105 minutes*). The entire time available during this period is allocated to the brief presentations of the procedure flow charts and the organization value analysis charts by the team captains. The number of teams participating in the seminar determines the time schedule for the period. These presentations are useful for both the teams themselves and the students in general. Additional learning is acquired by the students in reviewing the techniques applied, and the team that is making the presentation gains experience in presenting a project of this nature which will be helpful in the final project presentation to the company's top management. The instructor must control the length of each presentation and prohibit irrelevant questioning, arguing, and long-winded explanations. The total session time allows only cursory explanations during the presentations. After all the presentations have been made, the instructor should conduct a critique by highlighting the strong and the weak points of each presentation so that the final OVAC proposals will receive audience acceptance.

SEVENTH SESSION

1. *Creative Thinking; Guest Speaker* (*60 minutes*). Prior to this session, the seminar efforts were directed primarily to the data-collection aspects of the job plan information phase. Here the emphasis changes to analytical efforts. The creative thinking lesson objective is to explore the potential of human creativity. This is of particular importance because of the part it plays in VAMP. VAMP is based on defining the function of a procedure or organization and developing alternate methods to accomplish the function. The alternates are the items that result in increased value, and they are developed by the process of creative thinking.

During this period the guidelines for conducting a creative thinking or brainstorming session are reviewed. The elements of successful creative thinking are explained and the impediments are identified. Many examples are used to stress the importance of creative thinking, not only in relation to the seminar project, but in every attempt at achievement. Excellent presentations of this subject are available, most of which are based on Alex F. Osborn's book *Applied Imagination.**

2. *OVAC Analysis—Instructor (120 minutes)*. The remaining phases of the job plan are explained during this period, as is the use of the OVAC analysis sheet (Exhibit 9). Emphasis is placed on the following topics:

    a. Functional definitions for both basic and secondary functions.
    b. Development of functional alternates.
    c. The order of application; that is, organization, activity, and task.
    d. Evaluation of the alternates, including the establishment of value ratings.
    e. Solution and development of the best function alternate.
    f. Importance of making an excellent presentation of the proposal.

It is not unusual for the students and the instructor to feel that two hours are insufficient for an adequate explanation of OVAC analysis. However, two sessions of the same duration would prove just as inadequate. In guiding the discussion, the instructor must use particular care to avoid digressions.

3. *Procedure Flow Chart Analysis—Instructor (45 minutes)*. The analysis of a procedure flow chart generally follows the pattern explained in a previous lesson. Therefore, the period of instruction is adjusted accordingly. The lesson objective is to teach the students to use the principles and techniques of analysis in a slightly different manner.

The *blast-create-refine* technique of value engineering is introduced as the prime tool of procedure value analysis. The differences between the techniques and effects of traditional cost reduction and the techniques and effects of the functional approach using blast-create-refine should be explained and illustrated to emphasize the additional benefits of procedure value analysis. Class participation is obtained by using canned examples of procedure flow charts to demonstrate the technique.

EIGHTH SESSION

1. *OVAC Analysis; Project Work Instructor (120 minutes)*. During this period, the teams perform an analysis of their OVAC projects. By this time each team member has probably determined in his own

---

* Charles Scribner's Sons, New York, 1953.

mind what is wrong with the organization and what corrective action should be taken. These prejudgments are inevitable but seldom correct. The seminar instructor and project leaders must guide the teams to overcome these prejudgments and insure that—

    a. The basic function of each organization is properly chosen and defined in a two-word functional definition.
    b. The creative thinking phase develops a reasonable quantity of alternates which are recorded on the OVAC analysis sheet.
    c. The evaluation of the alternates is logical and thorough.
    d. The proper order of application is followed; that is, the organization's functions first, the highest-cost activity next, and finally the activities in order of priority of cost. If time permits, the analysis continues through all the high-cost tasks.

    2. *Procedure Flow Chart Analysis; Project Work—Instructor (105 minutes).* The OVAC analysis may not be completed by the end of the previous lesson. Nevertheless, the teams' efforts must be diverted to the procedure flow charts. This change usually motivates the teams to settle minor OVAC problems during nonseminar time. During this period the teams display their procedure flow charts and apply the blast-create-refine technique. The project leaders should make certain that all facets of this technique are used.

NINTH SESSION

    1. *Analysis; Project Work—Instructor (60 minutes).* This period is provided to allow additional time for the teams to complete the analysis of OVAC and the procedure flow chart and is a continuation of the preceding two classes.

    2. *Proposal; Chart Preparation—Instructor (165 minutes).* During this period the teams develop their OVAC and procedure flow chart proposals on wall charts. The project leaders should assist and the instructor must emphasize the importance of the proposal preparation. These proposals reflect the entire effort of the workshop seminar and should be constructed with this in mind. During the final session the team captains will present their projects to an audience of executives. Therefore, the wall charts for OVAC and the proposed procedure should not be unduly complex or detached. They should facilitate a brief oral description on a level easily understood by the uninitiated. Each team's OVAC presentation should include as a minimum a chart of the existing

organization, a chart of the proposed organization, and a basis for comparison. This basis can be the total cost of the existing and proposed organizations, or it can be the units of work now produced and the units of work that could be produced by the proposed organization. The procedure flow charts should be constructed in the same manner. A comparison of the existing and proposed procedures can be in terms of estimated cost. If no figures are available, a comparison of the quantity of discrete operations can be made. If the proposals are subsequently approved for implementation and more detailed charts are required, the team can reconvene and complete this work after the seminar has been concluded.

TENTH SESSION

1. *Presentation—Seminar Director (225 minutes)*. The last session does not have much learning value. Rather, its objective is one of motivation. The presentation session motivates the teams by affording them an opportunity to explain what they have accomplished to higher management. It is motivation by recognition. Hopefully, the audience will be motivated to further VAMP efforts after listening to the presentation and evaluating the results.

The seminar director should prepare well for this session, giving special attention to the following:

a. *Audience*. The management level of those attending will be determined in part by the management level of the students. In all cases, the next higher level should be invited to attend. The chief executive and his staff should receive invitations, as should any other individuals who could aid in the expansion of the VAMP effort. After the presentations, the audience should be solicited for comments and suggested improvements.

b. *Publicity*. The presentation should be treated as a special event and publicized. A bit of public relations can add import and assure full audience attendance. Articles in the company newspaper, bulletin board notices, and special invitations can contribute to a successful seminar presentation.

c. *Facility*. The presentation facility should be large enough to accommodate the audience in comfort, and provisions should be made for serving coffee and doughnuts. Training aids such as flip-chart easels, blackboards, or wall area where the large OVAC's and procedure flow charts can be mounted and removed rapidly are essential. If a proper setting is unavailable on company premises, the presentations should be scheduled at a nearby hotel or restaurant that has suitable facilities.

d. *Schedule.* The presentations must be brief, lively, and interesting, with the time allotted to each team dependent upon the number of teams in the seminar. It is recommended that the director conduct a rehearsal of the presentations on the evening preceding the final session to insure that the presentations are professional.

INDEX

Index

About the Author

WARREN J. RIDGE is the manager of value engineering for Control Data Corporation's Analog-Digital Systems Division in La Jolla, California. Prior to joining Control Data Corporation, he served with the Convair Division of General Dynamics as cost reduction and value control administrator for a period of five years. His background also includes management positions in production engineering, design engineering, and financial analysis. A graduate of Boston College, he later attended the Massachusetts Institute of Technology and the San Diego State College Graduate School. He is a member of the Society of American Value Engineers, past president of the San Diego Chapter, and technical chairman of the 1969 National SAVE Conference.